Foste
Iris

Foster's Book of Irish Murder

Allen Foster

NEW ISLAND

FOSTER'S BOOK OF IRISH MURDER
First published in 2018 by
New Island Books
16 Priory Hall Office Park
Stillorgan
County Dublin
Republic of Ireland

www.newisland.ie

This paperback edition published 2019.

Paperback ISBN: 978-1-84840-743-5
Hardback ISBN: 978-1-84840-606-3
Ebook ISBN: 978-1-84840-607-0

Typeset by JVR Creative India
Cover design by Karen Vaughan
Printed by Scandbook, Sweden.

New Island Books is a member of Publishing Ireland.

*For my friend and literary agent Jonathan Williams,
in grateful acknowledgement for all his hard work
over the years.*

Contents

Introduction

The act of murder is a terrible crime yet it never fails to fascinate. This is no different now than centuries ago. The more unusual or remarkable a murder is, the more it catches the public's attention. The murders detailed in *Foster's Book of Irish Murder* occurred in Ireland from the early eighteenth century to the mid-twentieth century and are all distinctive in some way or another.

Ireland has had its share of violent murders throughout the years and this collection of compelling cases details killings caused by greed, desperation, hatred, madness, jealousy and passion. The task of catching the perpetrators of these most heinous crimes fell to the authorities where the foul deeds took place. Local constables and volunteer watchmen policed their communities and detected crimes, and it was not until 1822 that the first organised police force came into being in Ireland. This was called the Royal Irish Constabulary, and after the foundation of the Irish Free State in 1922 this force was dissolved and replaced by An Garda Síochána (and by the Royal Ulster Constabulary in Northern Ireland).

Many of the murderers in this book were found guilty and hanged for their crimes, and the last person to be hanged in Ireland for murder was executed in 1954. In times past, justice moved swiftly. Trials usually took place a short time after the accused was arrested and, if found guilty and denied leave to appeal, the killer could expect to be hanged in as little as a few weeks after the verdict.

I researched the murders using numerous old books, magazines and newspaper articles as a start before looking online through digitized contemporary newspapers, ending up with files on the cases that were three phone books thick. From the case of a father who killed his children for life insurance money, to that of an opportunist who almost got away with the perfect murder, to a chilling motiveless killing, *Foster's Book of Irish Murder* recounts gripping cases from the dark side of Irish history.

The Bodkin Murders

The shocking massacre of an entire household of ten people – one of whom was a pregnant woman – that took place in 1741 at Carrowbawn House in County Galway would be an appalling crime in any age. The sheer brutality of the murders is still hard to fathom nearly 300 years later. The property lay 4 miles from Tuam on the Headford road and belonged to Oliver Bodkin, a wealthy landowner.

Bodkin married around 1720 and in time his wife gave birth to a son called John, who was commonly known as John FitzOliver to distinguish him from two other members of the family with the same Christian name. The child was his parents' delight and he was extravagantly pampered. Oliver Bodkin's wife died in 1730 and he remarried in 1732. A son was born to this second marriage in 1733 and called Oliver. According to custom, the infant was given to foster parents – a tenant, John Hogan, and his wife – for the first three years of his life. The child was raised alongside the Hogans' children and strong bonds were formed.

When he was 3 years old, Oliver was returned to his parents.

John Bodkin, the son from the first marriage, was later sent to Trinity College in Dublin to further his education. He was marked out for a career in law, but he neglected his studies and the path that had been chosen for him. He fell into bad habits and eventually quit Trinity and returned home to Carrowbawn House. John was jealous of the affection his father and stepmother displayed for young Oliver and grew to resent the child. John's father and stepmother frowned upon his wild behaviour and his abandonment of college, and a distance grew between them and the young man.

John's resentment of his stepmother and half-brother caused such ill-feeling in the household that he decided to leave Carrowbawn for good in 1737. The 17-year-old went to stay at the home of his uncle, who was also named John Bodkin: Carrowbeg House, a mile to the west of Carrowbawn. The uncle was a successful barrister and resided mostly in Dublin for work. His occupation led to him being popularly known as 'the Counsellor'. He had two sons, Patrick and John, who were known as Patrick FitzCounsellor and John FitzCounsellor. John and his sons only occasionally visited the property for a few weeks every year.

The house was looked after by another brother called Dominick. He is described as an unmarried, elderly rogue who had a notorious reputation and was an unsavoury individual. He was known as Blind Dominick, because he was blind in one eye. He had a fearsome appearance as his face had been scarred by smallpox in childhood. John FitzOliver lived at Carrowbeg House for the next four years with this unsuitable man as a companion, there to vent his grievances to, and to influence him.

The only notable incident recorded from this time happened in 1739, when the Counsellor's two sons visited Carrowbeg for a holiday. Patrick seemed to be in good health but he was found dead in bed one morning. As the death was not suspicious no investigation took place. In the spring of 1741 young John FitzOliver learned that his father had changed his will, leaving his entire estate to his second son, and disinheriting John entirely. He was furious. Around this time Oliver Bodkin confided to a friend, Lord Athenry, that his son had threatened to murder him.

John's anger at being disinherited consumed him and fuelled a terrible rage. In desperation, he decided his only choice was to kill his father, stepmother and half-brother. In Blind Dominick he found a willing ally. His former foster father, John Hogan, also agreed to help, as did a man called Roger Kelly. It is not stated why Dominick and Hogan were such willing accomplices to the terrible murders that followed. The conspirators dined at Carrowbeg House on 18 September 1741, and finalised their plan. They agreed that it was safer to put all to the knife or sword rather than use unreliable and noisy firearms. The four men met at Carrowbeg House the following night. As they prepared for their attack, Roger Kelly went outside on the pretext of checking his horse and fled.

Undeterred, the other three men made their way to Carrowbawn around midnight. The guard dogs met them in the yard, but they knew the men and did not bark. Expecting to be stroked, the dogs approached them – and the men cut their throats. The three men then entered the farmworkers' quarters and quietly asked one if Counsellor Bodkin had arrived and was staying in the house. The worker said he had not arrived and went back to sleep. John FitzOliver, Blind Dominick and John Hogan cut the throats of the two men and two boys there as they slept. There was no turning back now.

The three conspirators silently entered the house and killed another servant and his wife as they slept. Next John murdered a Galway merchant named Marcus Lynch who had come down for the Tuam races and was unlucky enough to be staying in Carrowbawn House on the wrong night. John Hogan entered the main bedroom and quietly cut the throats of John Bodkin and his wife, who was heavily pregnant. However, he lost his nerve when it came to killing 7-year-old Oliver, who was sleeping in the same room.

As John Hogan approached Oliver's bed the child awoke and, recognising his foster father, cried, 'Ah! Daddy, Daddy, sure you won't kill your little child!' Hogan quieted Oliver and warned him not to stir or he would be killed. He smeared the boy with blood so the others would think he was dead. But Blind Dominick entered the room, saw through the ruse and swore the boy must die. He threatened to kill Hogan if he did not murder the boy. Hogan, feeling he had no choice, sliced Oliver's throat open so violently that he cut off the boy's head, which he then placed on the body of his murdered father. Having butchered every person at the house, the murderers made off into the night.

The killings were discovered the next day, and a horrified crowd of locals gathered outside the house. John FitzOliver made his way to Carrowbawn and feigned grief over his father's corpse, but many were suspicious of him, especially since there were bloodstains on his clothes. On hearing of the dreadful murders, Lord Athenry hurried to the scene. Remembering that John had threatened to kill his father, Athenry immediately interrogated him. John's replies were so unconvincing that Athenry, who was a justice of the peace, arrested him and sent him to Galway Gaol under military escort. John confessed to the murders and gave the names of his accomplices, who had fled on hearing of his arrest.

John Hogan and Blind Dominick were quickly tracked down and thrown into Galway Gaol to await trial. John FitzCounsellor was also arrested on suspicion of involvement and held for trial. On 6 October 1741 the four men were brought to Tuam for the assizes, under heavy military escort. A grand jury was sworn in the following morning. The charges against John FitzCounsellor were thrown out, but the other three were then put up for trial.

A jury was sworn in and the trial got underway. John Hogan pleaded guilty, saying that he had killed the Bodkin family, but had wanted to save his foster child. Blind Dominick also pleaded guilty, as did John Bodkin. It took the jury only ten minutes to convict them, and the judge sentenced to hang the following day. It was customary at that time to hang murderers as close as possible to the place where they had committed the crime, and the three men were carted from Tuam to Carrowbawn next morning.

There, close to the road, John Hogan was hanged from a tree. Next was Blind Dominick. When John Bodkin's turn came, he addressed the assembled crowd. 'Two years before the murder of my father, another murder was committed by my cousin, John FitzCounsellor, of Carrowbeg, and it was that undiscovered crime that led me to commit the murder for which I am now about to die,' he told the stunned onlookers. 'He murdered his elder brother, Patrick, who left one son after him. On the night of that occurrence, Patrick and his brother, John … slept in the same room. In the middle of the night John FitzCounsellor rose from his bed, and putting a pillow across the face of his brother

Patrick, sat upon him, and thus smothered him. The death was unheeded at the time, inasmuch as the world had it that it was a sudden death.'

Having made his speech, Bodkin was hanged. His body and that of his uncle were hung in chains at the place of execution, to act as a warning to others. Hogan's head was cut off and placed on a spike on top of the market house in Tuam. John FitzCounsellor was at the execution, but fled on his horse after hearing his cousin's accusation. He evaded pursuers for a while by posing as a farm labourer, but was caught in a bog in Belcare on 22 October 1741.

Although he did not confess, after a brief trial in Galway on 8 March 1742, John FitzCounsellor was found guilty. He was hanged the following day at Gallows Green, beside the city walls. He was decapitated and his head was taken to Tuam to be placed in a cage on public display. Carrowbawn House was demolished in an effort to erase all trace of the terrible murders.

Lethal Lemonade

John Dunphy of Waterford suffered a terrible death on 19 December 1899. Eyewitnesses saw the 11-year-old boy in agony, clutching his stomach, on Beresford Street shortly before 2pm. As the youth collapsed, he foamed at the mouth and called out for his father. The boy went rigid in the arms of a man who tried to comfort him. A car was flagged down and the boy was rushed to Waterford County Infirmary. There a Dr Kelleher did all he could, but the boy suffered several fits and died a short while later.

The child's body remained rigid throughout, and he stayed conscious until the end. Dr Kelleher immediately thought he had been poisoned with strychnine. One of the nurses recognised the boy as the son of Patrick Dunphy, an elderly labourer from Yellow Road. The 74-year-old was no stranger to tragedy. His wife had died the previous year and another son, 9-year-old Edward, had died a few months before. Now, following John's death in similar circumstances, police became suspicious and made inquiries. On discovering that both boys had been insured, they arrested the elderly father.

Edward had died on the morning of 29 September after suffering from fits and foaming at the mouth. An inquest had concluded that he had died of natural causes, a severe epileptic attack having caused a heart attack. But a post-mortem examination of Edward and John's bodies revealed that both boys had been poisoned with strychnine, and Patrick Dunphy was charged with murdering his sons.

When the trial opened in Waterford on 9 March 1900, Dunphy pleaded not guilty. The prosecution contended that the accused had murdered both boys for the sake of a few pounds in insurance money. He had received £10 for Edward and would have collected that same amount again for John if the crime had not been detected. It was beyond doubt that Dunphy had purchased strychnine from two chemists in the city. Anticipating that Dunphy's defence might be that his sons had accidentally consumed strychnine bought to kill rats, or had been prone to suffering fits, the prosecution put Dunphy's 13-year-old daughter Mary on the stand.

'We have been living in the house for the last eight years, during that time we were never troubled by rats,' she told the court. 'My father never complained about rats.' Neither had he ever bought poison to kills rats, she said. Asked about the family's health, Mary simply declared: 'None of us ever had a fit.' She told the court that her father and another brother had been out of work for two weeks at the time of John's death. When she had asked her father for money to run the house, he said he had none. On the day of John's death her father had taken him out to buy him a new suit of clothes. 'They went off together, and John was in the best of humour,' Mary recalled sadly. 'That was the last I saw of John.' Her father came back in the afternoon 'roaring and bawling' and told her John was dead.

A cousin, Michael Brennan, testified that neither boy had been prone to illness or fits. Next to take the stand was Dr Kelleher, resident surgeon at the Waterford County

Infirmary, and he gave graphic details of John's agonising death. Men had brought the boy to the hospital and his father had arrived shortly afterwards, Dr Kelleher testified. The youth's body was rigid, his head thrown well back, his jaw and fingers clenched. When Dr Kelleher had asked his father if John had ever had a fit before, Dunphy had replied 'Once.' The doctor had advised him to get a priest, and Dunphy had left to find one.

John had been put to bed, and Dr Kelleher had tried to open his mouth to help him breathe. The boy suffered several severe fits before dying a short while later. 'His eyes were very prominent – a wild, glaring expression; his jaws firmly shut, the angles of his teeth visible,' Dr Kelleher concluded. 'I formed the opinion that the fit was most likely poisoning by strychnine.' The doctor testified that he had performed a post-mortem examination on the body with his colleague Dr Jackman, and had removed the organs and sent them to the Royal College of Surgeons in Dublin for examination.

A week later police had exhumed Edward Dunphy's corpse and his internal organs were also removed and sent to Dublin for examination. Dr Kelleher concluded his testimony by asserting that Dunphy had told him that John 'always had a bad head and the mother died shaking – he illustrated the motion with his hands. I asked the prisoner if the boy became unconscious in a fit, but do not remember the answer. I asked him if the boy had any moaning in these fits and he replied that he would begin to shake, but that he would not bite his tongue.'

Dr Jackman, who corroborated Dr Kelleher's evidence, said Dunphy's wife had died from cancer, and that she had never suffered from any fits while he attended her. Next the court heard from Professor Lepper of the Royal College of Surgeons, who acted as a government analyst in criminal cases. From his investigations he had concluded that somewhere between two and three grains of strychnine had been administered to John Dunphy, and that one or two grains had been given to his brother Edward. 'From a third of a grain to one grain and a half of strychnine is a fatal dose for a child of 9 or 10 years,' he said.

Other witnesses testified that the Dunphy household had never had a problem with rats and that the boys were both healthy. The court heard chilling testimony of Dunphy's calculating behaviour from Mrs Mary Cooney, who owned a public house on Parade Quay. She knew Dunphy and recalled him coming into the pub and asking for a half-glass of beer for himself and a bottle of lemonade, which he said was for a little boy outside the door. Mrs Cooney saw Dunphy take the glass of lemonade to the door, bring in the boy and give it to him, saying, 'Finish the lemonade, boy.' The boy took the glass and drank it, then handed the glass back to his father. Then they left.

Answering a question from the jury foreman, Mrs Cooney replied, 'He turned his back to me when he was giving the lemonade to the boy, but I saw nothing in his hand.' In response to a question from the judge, she said, 'Dunphy put the glass to his mouth when the boy had drunk it, and seemed to finish what was left.'

District-Inspector Smith gave evidence that Dunphy had made a statement the day after John's death in which Dunphy claimed his other son, Edward, had also died from fits, as had the boy's mother and grandfather. 'I believe it is engendered in the family,' Dunphy had said, adding that 'There was no talk of buying John clothes.' In the same statement, Dunphy claimed that his son must have accidentally taken poison that he had bought to treat his bad leg. 'I'll be hung, but I would rather be hung than be in jail for my life,' he said.

Patrick Dunphy refused to give evidence, but the defence urged the jury to be certain that he had been responsible for his sons' deaths and that they had not accidentally taken the poison themselves. In summing up the case, the judge directed the jury to consider the evidence carefully. He was particularly scathing of the practice of companies offering insurance on children's lives, but he told the jury that it did not matter if Dunphy had killed his children for insurance money, as long as proof of the crime was established. After retiring for only four minutes, the jury found the accused guilty of murder. The judge sentenced him to death.

Since the last execution in Waterford had been thirty-six years earlier, a gallows had to be erected inside the walls of the jail to hang the heartless father on the morning of 10 April 1900. On account of his age, many had expected Dunphy to be given life in jail, but his crime was so terrible that the authorities declined to offer him any mercy. Dunphy never confessed or repented, and he met his death with quiet resignation. The hangman carried out the execution with brisk efficiency, and death was instantaneous.

Justice Delayed

There have been cases where murderers have escaped detection for several years, only to be caught by mere chance. The strange story of Bernard McCann from Newtownhamilton, County Armagh is one of these.

In July 1813 he worked as a baker for Adam Sloane in Lisburn. This was a respectable trade and he earned a good wage of six shillings and six pence a week. McCann was about 20 years old, slightly built and had previously worked as a baker in Dromore, before entering Sloane's employment in May. When Sloane refused to allow him to attend the famous Maze race festival, which was held over several days, the headstrong youth quit his job on 22 July. The Maze races were incredibly popular – tens of thousands people flocked to them.

At the races he met Owen McAdam, a horse dealer from Keady, County Armagh. The pair may have already known each other, as Keady and Newtownhamilton lay close to each other. Perhaps the men met at McAdam's lodgings in Lisburn, where McCann sometimes stayed. In any case, on 21 July, Owen McAdam arrived in Lisburn for the race festival with two horses to sell and lodged at John Dawson's inn for a few nights. He and McCann befriended each other and were frequently seen together over the next few days.

Their movements on 25 July are particularly well-documented. After church, McAdam went into Frances McDonnell's inn in Hillsborough for breakfast. He later returned with McCann and another man for refreshments. She subsequently recalled that the trio had dinner and a few drinks before they departed at 4pm. Frances McDonnell had spoken with McCann and he had told her his name and where he was from. She also saw McAdam taking a bundle of notes out of his pocket, and saw a piece of ginger come out with them. She enquired what he did and he said he was a horse dealer.

Next McCann and McAdam went to the residence of John Chambers in Hillsborough around 5pm and tried to conclude a deal to sell him a grey 2-year-old colt of about 14 hands with a long tail. The animal was quite distinctive as it had a small cut on one leg caused by a kick from a horse at the fair, and a sore eye due to a bite from another. A deal could not be reached for the animal, although McCann urged his friend to sell as he wished to return to Lisburn and pick up his belongings before it got too late.

The pair told Chambers they intended to travel back to south Armagh together afterwards. During negotiations McAdams took a distinctive watch out of his pocket and John Chambers and his son Joe admired it. The watch had the figures of four soldiers painted on the face and they had never seen anything like it. McCann and McAdams departed before 6pm and next called in to James Rooney's inn at Lisburn, 5 miles away, at around 7pm. They had a drink and left the grey horse there while they went into the town to pick up McCann's belongings at John Dawson's inn and Adam Sloane's house. McCann told both men he intended to go to Dromore and return to his previous employer.

They returned to Rooney's inn around 10pm and ordered half a pint of spirits. There was a third man with them, but he remained outside. McCann filled a glass of spirits for McAdam, who was clearly drunk, but drank little himself. When this was finished he pressed a second glass on him. When Rooney protested that McAdam had already had enough to drink, McCann said it would sober him up. They left shortly afterwards with the horse, and McCann told Rooney he would safely see his friend into Hillsborough. That was the last time Owen McAdam was seen alive.

The next morning the body of a man was fished out of the Lagan canal at Newport bridge near Lisburn. It was clear the man had met a violent death and the authorities were called. An inquest was held later that day and several witnesses – including John Chambers and his son, Frances McDonnell, and James Rooney – gave evidence that they had seen the unknown man in company with Bernard McCann. A doctor testified that the dead man had been savagely hit on the head, then strangled and thrown in the canal. Nothing was found in the deceased's pockets except for a piece of ginger. The victim was described as around 30 years old and 5 feet 8 inches tall. He had been wearing a light blue coat.

A verdict of wilful murder by Bernard McCann was passed and a search for him commenced. He was described as a good-looking, well-dressed young man with fair hair, his pale complexion slightly marked by smallpox. In an effort to identify the unknown victim, the body was placed in an open coffin and left in the doorway of Lisburn Church on 27 July in the hope that someone would recognise him.

John Dawson came forward and informed the authorities the body was that of Owen McAdam from Keady, County

Armagh. Identity established, the body was interred in the graveyard. A soldier's wife passing through Lisburn, who had seen the body and heard the man's name, decided to find his family as she would be in Keady the following day. She must have been successful as Owen's father Patrick and another son arrived in Lisburn with a horse and cart on 30 July to take his body home for burial in the family plot.

Efforts were made to dissuade the men from exhuming the body, but the McAdams were not to be put off from their grim duty. They dug up the coffin Owen was buried in and placed the body in a coffin they had brought with them. Before they set out on their painful journey to Keady over 40 miles away, Owen's brother was persuaded to pay a visit to the Marquis of Downshire. The peer promised to do everything in his power to find Owen's murderer and gifted the young man a few guineas to help him and his father home.

The last sightings of Bernard McCann came on 26 July. At 5am two men with a grey horse called at the Red Cow Inn, which lay on the road between Lurgan and Portadown, and woke proprietor William Mills to get them breakfast. They offered the horse to him for a guinea but Mills was wary of the low price. When Mills later learned of the murder he realised that one of the men fitted the description of the wanted man. The men did not linger and continued on south towards Armagh. Later that day a man fitting Bernard McCann's description stopped with James Vance at Tanderagee and asked for a month's grazing for his grey colt with a long tail and a sore eye. They agreed a price of £1 and the man paid a small amount upfront, promising to return. The man offered to sell Vance his watch, which had pictures of soldiers on its dial. After these two sightings the trail grew cold.

It was not until ten years later that McCann was discovered by chance in Galway. In the fullest account of the McCann trial it is never said who discovered the fugitive, but the popular story is that a wandering pedlar, who had once been a baker in Lisburn and knew McCann, spotted him in Galway city in 1823. By now McCann, who was going by the name James Hughes, was a prosperous butcher and well-respected citizen. He was 29 years old and married with five children. He had amassed a fortune of £1,500 and owned 28 acres of land.

Although many years had passed and McCann was now a heavyset man of 17 stone, the pedlar was certain of his identity and reported it to the mayor of Galway, James Burke. The mayor, who had known 'Hughes' for years, found it hard to believe that a respectable man known for his generosity and good deeds was a murderer – but, to his credit, he took the allegations seriously. He confronted Hughes, told him he faced a serious accusation, and warned him that if he could not clear it up to his satisfaction, it would give him no pleasure, but he would have to detain him.

Hughes denied the allegations. He told Burke he was from Tyrone and that even if he had been drinking with the deceased, no one could prove he had murdered him. This was evidently not a satisfactory explanation for the mayor, who consequently had him imprisoned. Hughes was butcher to John Reilly, a collector of customs in the city, who visited him in jail shortly after his committal. Reilly told Hughes he was sorry to see him there. Hughes denied he was McCann and appeared to make light of his circumstances, explaining that he had been accused of murder and robbery. When Reilly asked where he was from, Hughes replied he was from Dungannon, County Tyrone. Reilly asked him if he knew the Knoxes and Hughes said he knew Hugh Knox. But Reilly knew all the Knox family, and there was no Hugh.

When it became apparent that the prisoner had a charge to face, he was brought north to Downpatrick and examined by County Down Magistrate Hugh Moore and the Marquis of Downshire. The Galway butcher could not substantiate his claim that he was from Dungannon. For a start, he did not know the names of several prominent people in the town or the names of any townlands adjoining it. When asked who kept the Head Inn, and the names of the Protestant and Roman Catholic clergymen, 'Hughes' said the name of the innkeeper was Reid, and the names of the clergymen were Gill and Maher. No one by these names had ever been known in the town. Furthermore, no one by the name of McCann or Hughes had ever lived in Dungannon.

McCann was formally charged with the murder of Owen McAdam and remanded in custody until the trial, which took place in Downpatrick on 29 July 1823. Even though it had been more than ten years since the murder and inquest. all the original witnesses were still alive and gave evidence in court. Their testimony was damning and there was little doubt what the verdict would be.

McCann could produce no witnesses to back up his claim that he was James Hughes, but the prosecution had several declare he was Bernard McCann of Newtownhamilton who had been seen with Owen McAdam before his death. The judge summed up the case for two hours before giving it to the jury. After an hour's deliberation they found McCann guilty, but they recommended mercy on account of his subsequent good conduct.

Addressing the guilty man, the judge said that although the evidence was circumstantial and had been produced after a lapse of many years, there was no doubt in his mind that the verdict was proper: McCann had cruelly murdered poor McAdam for his money. The judge gave thanks that the killer had been brought to justice, and sentenced him to death by hanging. McCann asked for a 'long day' – a now-forgotten term for a longer respite between sentence and execution, so that he could say goodbye to his wife and children – but the judge refused to grant him even this small mercy. McCann was executed outside Downpatrick Gaol two days later on 31 July.

On the scaffold, McCann admitted his guilt and sought forgiveness for his crime. His execution was notable for going badly wrong. When the trap was pulled, McCann fell, but not to his death. The rope snapped and he dropped 20 feet to the ground. He landed on his feet, but with his arms pinioned, he fell backwards to the ground.

Soldiers carried him back inside the prison to wait while a stronger rope was procured. Stunned by the shock of the fall, it took the condemned man a few minutes to recover. He sat upright on his own coffin and asked for a drink of water. He remained sitting there for an hour and a half until the hanging could proceed, and then he calmly walked to the scaffold. He was more afraid of another fall than of death, but this time the execution proceeded smoothly.

The Wicked Lady

Captain John Peck was married to a popular novelist but he did not live with her. Instead, he kept a home on Portland Place in Dublin with his beautiful 19-year-old lover, Mary Bailis. One day, Peck met Bridget Butterly, who was also 19, on the street and made inappropriate advances towards her. She rebuffed him at first, but Peck was persistent. The next day, he approached her again, and this time he convinced her to become a servant in his home, promising an easy life and good money.

Butterly moved into his house at Portland Place, became his lover and fell pregnant. When she miscarried, Peck fired her, using the spurious excuse that she had made ill-advised remarks about members of his family. To make matters worse he refused to provide her with a reference, cruelly leaving her unable to find another job as a servant in any respectable household.

Butterly went to lodge at a house in Summer Hill, where she befriended another lodger, 21-year-old Bridget Ennis, who proposed they leave for England together to seek a better life. Butterly agreed and suggested they rob Captain Peck's house to get funds for the journey. She knew he kept large sums of money in a small writing desk. On 28 March 1821 they watched and waited until Peck and a servant called Edward

A very familiar figure.

Captain Peck meets Bridget Butterly.

Connor left the house to go into the city, leaving only Mary
Bailis and Eliza Connor, a servant woman, in the house.

Bridget Ennis, who was unknown to the women, knocked
on the door, and Mary Bailis let her in. Ennis explained that

she was a servant of the Henry Street apothecary Hunt and had been sent to Captain Peck's house to let them know that he had been run over by a hackney coach in North Earl Street and had broken both his legs. The injured man had been carried to Hunt's and requested that a messenger be sent to his home to ask that the women come to him.

The women believed Ennis's lies and were very upset. Mary decided to stay and mind her child, but sent Eliza to Captain Peck. Eliza did not know the way, so Ennis offered to show her the way. They set out at once, but when they reached Mountjoy Square Ennis said she had to go to Drumcondra as a child of Mrs Hunt's was being nursed there. She gave directions to Eliza and then left her to find her way.

Eliza found Hunt's where, to her surprise, no one knew anything of Captain Peck or any accident. She checked several other nearby apothecaries but drew a blank. Meanwhile, Ennis doubled back to rendezvous with Butterly and the went back to Portland Place.

'What will happen to us if we do anything to the young lady, Biddy?' asked Butterly.

'I would kill ten rather than be taken,' answered Ennis.

'But what will happen to my father and mother if I do it?' asked Butterly.

'How can we be discovered if we go to England?' replied Ennis.

Butterly went up and knocked on the door. Mary Bailis answered and warmly welcomed her into the house. They went into the parlour and chatted while Butterly cradled Mary's 2-year-old child. Soon Ennis knocked at the door and Mary allowed her in. As Mary's attention was with Ennis, Butterly put down the child and used a handkerchief to gag Mary at

THE BODY OF LETTY THOMPSON LAY ON THE HEARTH.

Mary Bailis's body is discovered.

Ennis's urging to prevent her calling for help. Then Butterly began dragging the poor woman downstairs into the kitchen.

Mary called out to Ennis for help, but Ennis merely said, 'Biddy, don't injure the young lady.' Butterly replied that she had no intention of hurting her. Ennis quickly grabbed three silver spoons and a black leather trunk with some of Mary's clothes in it and left the house. No sooner had Ennis closed the door behind her than Butterly pushed Mary down the final steps into the kitchen and, in a fit of jealous rage, picked up a poker and repeatedly hit her with it.

Butterly later admitted that she had hit Mary twice in the head with the poker while she and her victim both screamed.

'The blood gushed out in torrents' and then Mary lay still, she confessed. 'I stooped forward over her, and endeavoured to raise her up in my arms in an unaccountable impulse.' By now Butterly's clothes were covered with Mary's blood and she realised it was time to leave before she was discovered. She left the body where it lay and went upstairs. She met the child at the top of the stairs and picked it up and kissed it, then set it down in the parlour.

Butterly went upstairs, found Peck's writing desk, took it with her, and fled. When she returned to their lodgings in Summer Hill she was surprised that Ennis was not there waiting for her and worried she had been arrested. Butterly ran back to Portland Place, but came away when she saw Edward Connor, Eliza's husband, knocking on the door. Arriving back at her lodgings again, she found Ennis waiting for her. Ennis explained that she had taken the long way back to avoid meeting Eliza, who would by then have known she had been deceived and would almost certainly have recognised the stolen trunk.

Edward Connor arrived back at Portland Place before 3pm and knocked at the door. To his surprise, nobody answered. He knocked again, and while he waited he saw the child standing at the parlour window. It was crying and there was blood on its clothes and face. Connor had been standing at the door for five minutes when his wife returned to the house after her misadventures. They knocked again and there was still no answer so Eliza went over to the parlour window.

Knowing it was not on a catch, she pushed up the sash window from the outside, climbed inside, and then let her husband in. Eliza went down the stairs to the kitchen and saw the body of Mary Bailis lying in a hellish pool of blood.

At first it was thought Mary Bailis had killed herself, but a police surgeon quickly saw she had been brutally beaten to death. Captain Peck returned home at 4pm, saw a huge crowd gathered in front of his house, and learnt the dreadful news.

Peck gave the police a detailed account of what had been stolen. His writing desk had contained a bill of exchange for £300, a £20 note, a £10 note, and several £5 notes, along with an envelope containing £47. Few could believe that a woman could be murdered in a Dublin house in the middle of the day and her cries for help not be heard. It was clear she had been murdered between 1pm and 3pm, and that the murderers had escaped without leaving a trace.

That evening, the murderers were caught thanks to an eagle-eyed member of the public. Before 6pm Bridget Butterly went into a public house in Great Britain Street and asked to buy a small amount of tea and sugar and a quart of whiskey. She tendered a 30-shilling note in payment, but the assistant noticed she also had a blood-stained £10 note in her hand and asked her where she had got it.

Butterly replied that she had got it in exchange for a £5 note in another public house. Apparently she was illiterate and did not know the value of the money. The assistant was suspicious and voiced his concerns to his master. They held her and sent for the police. Butterly was taken to a nearby police station and searched. There was some blood on her bonnet, and, under her apron, her gown was covered in blood. She was also carrying £47 in an envelope. She tried to explain the blood by saying she had had a nosebleed and said Bridget Ennis had given her the money.

Butterly was brought to Portland Place, where she was immediately recognised and arrested. Police went to the lodgings in Summer Hill, arrested Ennis, and discovered the rest of Peck's stolen property. The three silver spoons were found on Ennis, and the writing desk was found smashed open under a bed. The leather trunk was found empty as Ennis had already pawned the clothes. Both women were charged with theft and the murder of Mary Bailis and remanded in custody in Kilmainham Gaol.

The two women faced trial on 2 May 1821. Butterly was described as pretty. One report says she was 'mild-looking, rather short in stature, and of a soft expression of countenance'. Ennis was described as an older-looking woman, 'more bold and confident in demeanour'. The jury brought in a verdict of guilty after only a quarter of an hour's deliberation.

The judge sentenced them to hang two days later. Bridget Butterly made a full confession, exonerating Ennis of the murder. But this was not enough to save Ennis. Both women were publicly executed at 2pm at Kilmainham Gaol, to the delight of a 3,000-strong crowd of men, women and children that had gathered to witness the gruesome spectacle.

Death in the Playground

The brutal murder of a 27-year-old teacher by schoolboys in an Irish town gathered considerable newspaper coverage worldwide in 1912, John Kelly was attacked and killed in Trim Industrial School in County Meath on 12 February of that year. The school was based in a site that had served as the town jail until 1890. Several Meath towns had joined together and decided to establish a school there for orphans and the children of parents in the various county workhouses.

The teaching staff there consisted of a headmaster and three assistant masters. Kelly, who was from Rush, County Dublin, joined as an assistant master in 1905. At any time the number of boys there ranged from 120 to 150, and they stayed until they reached the age of 16 and had learned a trade. Eight boys, five of whom were under 16, were brought before Resident Magistrate R.F. Olphert in Trim police barracks in connection with Kelly's killing: Thomas Reilly, Patrick O'Hara, Peter Tuite, Philip Farrelly, William Smith, Patrick Cox, James Brennan and John Conlon.

The large scrubbing brushes, hurley sticks, and heavy crooked sticks that were used to attack Kelly were displayed in the court. The inquest began with testimony from Samuel Kelly (no relation to the deceased), who had been headmaster of the school for twenty-two years. It was John Kelly's duty after suppertime, at 6.30pm, to supervise the boys in the yard, and he was doing this on the evening of his death. Samuel Kelly was making a round of the school, as usual, sometime before 7pm when he noticed an unusual stillness in the boys' yard. There was a lamp there and he could see the boys clustered under a shed and went to them.

'Boys, what's up?' he asked, but there was no reply. He looked at them for a minute, repeated the question, and then looked round and saw a figure lying under the shed. Kelly was dazed for a moment then ran to the prone figure and saw that it was John Kelly. Lying on his left side, he was unconscious but still breathing. Blood was gushing from his head and his face was swollen. The headmaster exclaimed 'Poor Mr Kelly!' when he realised the unfortunate man was beyond assistance.

The headmaster got his housekeeper to stay with Kelly while he sent a porter for a priest, a doctor, and the police and sought the help of nuns from the local convent. John Kelly was carefully stretchered to the workhouse hospital. He was still alive by the time Dr Reilly arrived but died shortly afterwards.

When the headmaster did a roll call there were two boys missing, he told the inquest: Thomas Reilly and Patrick O'Hara. All the other boys who were in the shed were ordered to bed. He added that John Kelly was a slightly built man and not very strong.

'Was John Kelly a humane and kind master to the boys under him?' enquired the magistrate.

'Yes,' replied the headmaster.

'And do you know anything which would account for this terrible tragedy?' the magistrate asked.

Kelly replied that he thought that it had something to do with playing hurley in the boys' yard, and about tea being stolen from the porter's lodge.

'He never chastised the boys in such a way that they would do anything?"

'No.'

'If anything happens in the school of a serious nature would it not be his duty to report to you?'

'It would.'

'And he would not inflict punishment himself?'

'No. I never knew of him to report anything to me during the whole time he was there.'

'And so far as you know he was popular with the boys?

'I would have thought he would be the last that the boys would interfere with.'

'I asked you these questions because it would be gratifying to his friends. There is really no motive that you can ascribe for this thing except some trifling matter?'

'No. I really do not think that Mr Kelly, as far as I can remember now, ever reported anything of any serious nature … When he was on duty I was never anxious.'

When questioned by the county coroner, D.J. Corry, the headmaster testified that one of the boys had been caught in the porter's room by the deceased and had been searched. In a pocket, John Kelly had found a key he had previously lost.

The headmaster added that he had always considered Kelly a great favourite in the school with the boys. The coroner noted that the deceased had been in charge of forty boys, and that it was usual for one person to be in that position.

Evidence was next heard from boys from the school. Seven-year-old Joseph Hart testified that it had been common talk at lunchtime that Kelly was to be beaten. He had heard Reilly, Tuite and O'Hara ask Cox that morning if he was ready to hit Kelly, and Cox had replied that he was.

Hart said he was in the shed in the boys' yard when Kelly came into the yard. The boys were standing in a line and had hurley sticks, scrubbing brushes, and sweeping brushes in their hands. When Kelly walked up the shed and then turned to go back, Reilly hit him on the head with a large scrubbing brush, Kelly fell down and then a lot of other boys rushed in to hit him with hurleys and brushes.

Hart said he saw Smith, Tuite and Farrelly hit Kelly with hurley sticks. Cox had a stick, but Hart did not see him hit Kelly. He saw O'Hara hit Kelly in the chest with a scrubbing brush and continue hitting him until the other boys ran away.

His older brother Edward corroborated his evidence, adding that the boys had planned to beat Kelly since the morning time. He had heard one of them say to the others, 'Are you ready for the lion's den tonight?'

Edward said he had seen O'Hara, Tuite, Cox, and Brennan run in at the deceased but had not seen them hit him. He added that he thought Kelly had been hit ten times. Edward believed Kelly had walked down the shed to see if the boys would touch him. When the coroner asked if he thought Kelly went there to show he was not afraid of the boys Edward replied, 'Yes.'

Terence Martin also testified that he had seen Reilly hit Kelly with the heavy scrubbing brush. After the teacher had fallen, he had seen O'Hara, Tuite and Smith hit him also, but had not seen Cox or Brennan hit Kelly. Martin testified that he had been threatened with a kicking by Cox and told to get a tar brush from the carpenter's shop at 4pm. They had planned to burn it in the yard to bring out Kelly.

Medical testimony was heard that Kelly's death was caused by shock and haemorrhage from his injuries, and that he had died within half an hour of receiving them. Other evidence was heard concerning the attack and the premeditated nature of it. Ill feeling had been brewing against Kelly since at least that morning, and he was well aware of it, and of the threat of violence against him that night.

In the morning he had told the boys, 'If you think you have a coward in me you are mistaken. I will be down in the yard tonight, and I will see who will touch me,' or words to that effect. The coroner concluded the inquest by addressing the jury about the considerable premeditation leading to Kelly's death. After half an hour's deliberation they found that John Kelly had died from injuries inflicted on him by the eight boys. Five of them were charged with his murder and three with manslaughter.

The trial was held a few weeks later, and the judge said the jury could find the five boys accused of murder guilty of the lesser charge of manslaughter if they saw fit. Peter Tuite and William Smith were found guilty of manslaughter and sentenced to three years in jail. Patrick Cox and Patrick O'Hara were found guilty of manslaughter and were sentenced to twelve months' imprisonment with hard labour. Philip Farrelly and John Conlan were found not guilty.

James Brennan was discharged, there being no evidence against him. Thomas Reilly was tried separately from the others, found guilty of manslaughter, and sentenced to three years in a reformatory. When no reformatory would accept him, this sentence was altered to two years' imprisonment with hard labour. He had only just turned 16.

Was John Kelly attacked for trivial reasons or was there a darker motivation for the boys' hatred of him? The defence asked one witness if 'any of the boys were in dread that Mr Kelly would do anything to them that night'. The witness replied, 'They did not want him to come among them.' When asked if John Kelly was popular with the boys, the same witness said he was not.

At this point the judge warned the defence that he was 'taking a dangerous line of defence in suggesting motive of this kind'. In summing up, the defence reminded the jury of the kind of 'human material that drifted into the control of these industrial schools'.

John Kelly's mother had the body of her only child interred in Whitestown graveyard in Rush, and she erected a headstone to the memory of 'her beloved son John who was murdered at Trim Industrial Schools, Feby 12th, 1912, aged 27 years'.

Buried Alive

The brutal murder of James Keys by his son John took place on 23 April 1822 in the townland of Shane, near Church Hill, County Fermanagh. On that day, father and son left their home together with their spades to dig a ditch some distance away from the house. They appeared to be on their usual good terms.

In the evening only John returned home, carrying both spades. Asked where his father was John said he had gone to look for a strayed goat. He later suggested that his father had gone to look for John's older brother Thomas, who was in the army and was quartered 10 miles away. Thomas had not been home for five weeks prior to his father's disappearance. John ate a hearty supper and went to bed. His mother, a sister, and a younger brother stayed up to await James's return.

When he did not return that night or the next day the family were alarmed but did nothing for fear their landlord would call in his debt if it became known that James Keys had disappeared. John's sister Ann was openly suspicious of his involvement in their father's disappearance and told him 'there would be more about it'. He merely replied that 'he did not value her'.

James's brother John had strong suspicions surrounding his disappearance and decided to organise a proper search on

THE CORPSE WAS STARK NAKED WHEN DISCOVERED.

James Keys's body is discovered.

May Day. He called at his missing brother's house at sunrise, saw his niece, and informed her of his intentions. His nephew and namesake came out of the house and repeated his claims that his father had gone to look for a goat or to look for his brother in the army. John and Ann went out with their uncle and two other people to make a search.

The body was found in on the mountainside in a newly dug ditch, 8 steps long, that was not connected to a nearby drainage ditch. When they were digging up the ditch John Keys was on a nearby hill in view. James's brother dug deep into the ditch and uncovered the naked corpse of his brother face down in the earth. It was clear that James had been murdered as there were marks of violence on his head and neck.

John Keys went in search of his nephew after making the gruesome discovery and saw him walking by the lough in conversation with a friend. Seeing his uncle approach John guessed that the body had been discovered and jumped into the lough. He stood there with the water up to his shoulders and swore he would drown himself.

He refused to come out of the water and shouted to his uncle: 'You accuse me of killing my father. I will never stand on green ground again. No one shall cast up to me that I killed my father!' He remained in the lough for over two hours and all efforts to get him to come ashore failed.

When John Keys and the others moved away from the water's edge his nephew would get out of the lough, but when they returned he would go in again out of reach. He began to make his will while up to his shoulders in the lough, though it was apparent he had no intention of drowning himself. He remained in the lough until a neighbour, William Collum, who could swim, arrived on the scene and fetched him out of the water.

The younger John Keys was conveyed to the house of local magistrate Captain John Faucett to be questioned. There he confessed to minor involvement in the murder and tried to shift the blame to his older brother Thomas. John claimed Thomas had approached him the day before their father's death and they had agreed to kill him and split his property between them. John's attempts to implicate his brother as the principal criminal party were immediately disproved and an inquest held by the county coroner quickly came to the conclusion that the deceased had met his death due to blows inflicted on him by his son John.

In an age when justice was usually carried out fairly quickly after a criminal had been caught, John Keys did not face trial until the Enniskillen Assizes on 21 March 1823.

He would have remained in the town's jail until then. The prosecution's evidence established the facts of the case. But one piece of testimony was particularly shocking. Surgeon Leonard had examined James Keys' body at the place it was found and related his findings to the court. He held that the deceased had two wounds. One, over the eye, had been made with a blunt weapon, while another, on the back of the head near the neck, had been made with a sharp weapon. Also, two ribs were fractured.

Leonard said that while these wounds might have been the cause of the deceased's death, he had seen men with worse wounds recover. Questioned by the judge, Leonard said he believed that Keys had been knocked unconscious by the heavy blows and then buried in the ditch while still alive. The jury retired for nearly half an hour and then returned with a guilty verdict. The judge sentenced Keys to be executed by hanging in two days and advised him to make the best use of the short time remaining for penance and prayer.

After he had been sentenced to death, young John Keys broke down, tearfully admitted his guilt, and confessed that he alone had carried out the crime and had falsely accused his brother of involvement, although he had nothing to do with the murder.

John Keys was hanged at 1pm on 23 March at Enniskillen Gaol, in front of a huge crowd of spectators. Appearing suitably penitent and resigned to his fate, Keys confessed his guilt in a few words to the crowd and repeated that none of his family had any part in his terrible crime. After allowing the condemned man to say some prayers, the executioner proceeded to do his duty.

The Perfect Victim

James McParland was an American tourist travelling around Ireland by himself in 1965 when he befriended his would be killer by chance. To this person, McParland was the perfect victim in every way: rich, travelling alone and only in sporadic touch with his family. No one would miss him for a long time. McParland's murder would have remained unsolved if it had not been for determined detective work and a stroke of luck.

McParland was from a wealthy background. He had fought in World War II and served with honour, but had returned home a different person and suffered from poor mental health. After his father died in 1947, James's health worsened. He was in and out of various mental institutions for many years until he was released to his brother's care in 1964.

Worried about James's health, his father had divided his estate between James and a brother and sister, but had established a trust fund with James's $20,000 share and invested it with the Northern Trust Company in Chicago on his behalf. James's brother was entrusted with looking after his welfare. In 1965 James seemed to have recovered his mental health and set about regaining his independence and life. He went to court and successfully won control of his inheritance.

The idea of taking a long holiday appealed to 48-year-old McParland, and he announced that he intended to travel for a couple of years. His brother and sister tried to talk him out of the trip, but he paid them no attention. He intended to make a leisurely tour of Ireland and bought a red Volkswagen car and a large aluminium Airstream caravan and arranged for them to be shipped over to Dublin.

McParland set out in June, flying to Europe to revisit places where he had served during the war. His family received postcards from France and Germany and then one from Ireland in August, announcing his arrival in Dublin. That was the last they ever heard from him. When James failed to send a birthday card to his brother in October, as was always his custom, the family became concerned and decided to make certain he was all right. The Northern Trust Company told them James had withdrawn half of his remaining money in August and deposited it with the Provincial Bank of Ireland. On the advice of local police in America, James's brother wrote to the Irish police and asked them to make sure no harm had come to him, outlining his concerns for James's welfare.

The enquiry was treated seriously and Detective Sergeant Timothy Farrell was tasked with tracking down the missing American tourist. Armed with a photograph and description of McParland he set about retracing his steps. The Dublin branch of the Provincial Bank of Ireland confirmed that McParland had called in to the bank in August and September and withdrawn £500 in cash on each occasion.

The cashier who dealt with the chatty American remembered him and told Farrell the first amount was to furnish the caravan and the rest was spending money as McParland was leaving Dublin. Farrell learned that McParland had stayed in one of Dublin's best hotels for several weeks, parking his caravan in the hotel garage while he fitted it out for his tour.

The gregarious, generous American made many friends in the hotel and they were sorry to see him go in the second week of September. McParland told no one where he planned to travel, but since he had bought scuba gear Farrell guessed that he intended to go diving along the east coast while the weather was still warm. Farrell checked every quaint coastal village hotel and pub and tourist site, and doggedly followed McParland's trail south.

Everywhere the friendly American had stopped with his distinctive caravan he was remembered. He had stayed for several days at Wicklow town to go scuba diving, as Farrell had guessed. In a Wexford pub, Farrell made a startling discovery: McParland had been travelling with someone. The publican described this companion as being in his forties, slim and narrow-faced with greying black hair and a small moustache. He thought the man might be from northern England.

The men seemed to be the best of friends and asked the best road to Waterford before they left. Farrell tracked the pair to a hotel in Waterford city, where the unknown man had signed his name 'C. Wilson, Dublin'. Next the pair stayed in a Dungarvan hotel for several days, and then they moved on to Cork, basing themselves in an upmarket hotel for several days while they visited the local tourist attractions.

Farrell noted that McParland paid for everything wherever the men stayed. The hotel happily cashed a £500 cheque for McParland as he had already spent his travelling money. But

Farrell discovered that McParland had not paid the hotel bill. Instead, Wilson had paid it in cash on 8 October, explaining that McParland had gone to buy petrol and they were leaving at once.

Detective Farrell followed their route to Limerick but had great difficulty tracking the American with the distinctive caravan. Previously it had been an easy task. Farrell checked several hotels and pubs in the Limerick area before he finally found a publican who remembered the American. He had come in, made a phone call, and had a few drinks at the bar. Saying he was James McParland from Chicago, he asked if he could cash a £50 cheque on his Dublin bank account.

As it happened the publican had not had £50 on hand and was unable to oblige the man. He told Farrell he was certain that McParland was alone. When shown the missing man's photograph he scanned it carefully and remarked that although a month had passed, he was certain the man in the photograph was not the man he had met, although there was a certain resemblance.

Farrell drove back to Garda headquarters in Dublin convinced that harm had come to James McParland and another man was using his car and caravan and impersonating him. It was clear that this man slightly resembled the missing man and was trying to withdraw his money. No doubt he would try again. An alert was issued to gardaí nationwide asking that they look out for the distinctive left-hand-drive red Volkswagen and large aluminium caravan and apprehend the driver.

In mid-January 1966, the Provincial Bank of Ireland informed gardaí that they had received a cheque for £700 signed by 'James R. McParland' from a Belfast bank looking for payment. They had compared the signature with a file sample and believed the cheque was a forgery. They had refused to honour it. When the forged cheque was compared to Wilson's signature, a handwriting expert declared that they had been written by the same person.

An investigation revealed that the mysterious Wilson had traded in the Volkswagen and caravan and a cheque for £700 to a Belfast car dealer for a new Volvo car the previous week. Detective Farrell verified that the Belfast 'McParland' matched the description of the man seen by the Limerick publican. Efforts to find this man continued but proved fruitless.

Several weeks later, the Northern Trust Company in Chicago alerted gardaí that a man in Belfast claiming to be James McParland had twice telegraphed the bank seeking to have the remaining money on deposit transferred to McParland's account with the Provincial Bank of Ireland. He had also telephoned the bank to try to persuade them to transfer the money, but the bank official did not believe he was McParland as the caller spoke with a British accent, and could not answer simple questions about McParland's family. So he refused to move any money.

Efforts to find the fake McParland and the Volvo car in Belfast came to nothing. The investigation ground to a halt and Farrell went on to other duties. When McParland's brother did not receive a birthday card from him in October 1966 he debated going over to Ireland to undertake a search himself. Instead, he sought the help of the US State Department, which formally requested the help of the Irish government to establish James McParland's whereabouts.

As the person with most knowledge of the case, Sergeant Farrell was reassigned to it. Rereading his notes from the previous year with fresh eyes, Farrell was drawn to the notes he had made of the conversation with the Limerick publican, who had spoken with the mysterious man impersonating McParland. The man had told him the imposter had made a phone call in the pub, and Farrell wondered who he had called. He drove to Limerick and re-interviewed the publican to see if could remember anything about the call.

Fortunately, the publican's memory was good. He recalled that the man had to wait for a connection, so he thought he must have been calling England. He was certain the man had spoken with a woman, and he had heard him say 'Hello Darling.' The publican had not heard anything else, but it was enough to set Farrell pondering whether the man had also rung the same number from the upmarket hotel in Cork, where the phone calls from his room would have been noted and charged on his bill.

Lucky for Farrell, the hotel had retained its records, which showed that the man had made three phone calls to the same number in Glasgow. The number was listed to a Charles Edward Wilson, and the Glasgow police were asked to arrest him. They found 43-year-old Wilson at home with his wife. Outside the modest house was the Volvo car he had bought in Belfast. On 6 November Inspector Hogan from Cork arrived in Glasgow, and charged Wilson with the murder of James McParland.

After speaking with his wife, Wilson agreed to waive extradition, and he flew back to Dublin with Hogan that same day. A few days later he led gardaí to a secluded spot nearly 12 miles south of Cork city on the road to Kinsale. He quickly pinpointed a location a short distance from a lay-by, and soon the body of James McParland was exhumed from a 3-foot-deep grave. The remains were mostly skeletal as Wilson had spread lime over the body to speed up its decomposition.

Wilson admitted to killing McParland while the pair were shooting game near Watergrasshill in Cork. He was later convicted of murder and jailed for life.

The Body in the Dung Heap

Joseph Fee was a 21-year-old butcher who lived with his family in Clones, County Monaghan, on the corner of Jubilee Street and Fermanagh Street. He ran a slaughter house in his backyard, which made him deeply unpopular with his neighbours. It smelt bad. Matters were made worse by the fact that he had a dung heap in the backyard too.

The smell became so offensive by December 1903 that the town council ordered Fee to remove the dung heap. On 15 December, he hired two men, Albert McCloy and John Farmer, to shift it. They spent the day laboriously forking the dung onto carts and drawing it out of the town. Fee told the men to leave a small amount behind for his garden. They were piling a small mound up against a wall, as requested, at about 4.30pm in the fading light of day when Farmer's fork struck something solid. They set about digging out the obstruction.

To their surprise, they revealed a boot – and then a man's foot. They immediately reported their find to the police, who rushed to the scene; under their direction, a man's body was recovered. The police at once suspected that it was John Flanagan, a 25-year-old egg dealer, who had been missing for eight months.

Flanagan had lived with his father Patrick and sister Anne just outside Clones, and the family bought eggs from local farmers and sold them to shops in Belfast. He was last seen at lunchtime on 16 April 1903 on a Clones fair day. He had left home that morning carrying the considerable sum of £70. Arriving in Clones he met his assistants Patrick Moan and Joseph Connolly and the trio set up their stall for the day.

At 10.30am, Flanagan met Joseph Fee, who owed him money. Fee asked Flanagan to call at his house at 11am, saying he would pay him then. But when Flanagan called, there was no one there. He waited for an hour for Fee, then returned to the stall to help load his pony and trap with eggs to be taken to the train station to catch the train to Belfast. At 12.30pm, the three men were busy buying eggs and loading up when Fee arrived, apologised for not being at home earlier and asked Flanagan to accompany him home so he could pay.

Flanagan set off down Fermanagh Street with Fee, telling Moan and Connolly that he would be back in ten minutes. When he did not return Moan went to look for him but could not find him. By now farmers were gathered around the stall looking for payment for the eggs John Flanagan had collected from them, so Moan sent word to Patrick Flanagan to come and pay the outstanding monies. Moan and Connolly then took the eggs to the station, before returning to look for John.

Patrick and Anne arrived in Clones in the early afternoon and a fresh search was made through the town – including every public house, as John liked a drink. Shocked by her brother's uncharacteristic disappearance, Anne feared the worst. Fee was among those who helped look for the missing man, telling Anne he had paid John the £2 he owed him in a public house and had not seen him since. He even suggested to Moan that Flanagan might have gone off with a woman. His disappearance was reported to the police, but their efforts to find him came to nothing.

John Flanagan's body is found.

The discovery of a body in Joseph Fee's yard eight months later instantly made him a person of interest. The body was recognised from clothes as that of John Flanagan. Within five minutes, police went to Fee's house and arrested him as he appeared to be about to flee. When police removed the body they found that the corpse was in remarkably good condition given that it had been covered in quicklime to speed its decomposition. The peaty soil in which it had been buried had counteracted the effects of the lime and preserved the body.

The corpse was removed to a nearby public house and the following day an inquest was held. Medical evidence concluded that John Flanagan had met a violent death. The cause was a violent blow to the head delivered with a sharp instrument which had penetrated the brain. Flanagan's throat had also been cut, and a cruel-looking pig-sticker knife had fallen from the corpse when it was exhumed.

It was as if poor John Flanagan had been slaughtered like an animal. The hole in his skull could have been made by an instrument used to kill animals in Fee's slaughterhouse, and the knife was identified as one of Fee's. The body had been buried only a few feet from the slaughterhouse.

Despite the evidence against him, and the obvious motive of robbery, Flanagan was tried twice – in March and July – and the two juries, made up of Monaghan natives, were unable to agree a verdict. A third trial commenced on 1 December at Belfast's Crumlin Road Court. A vast crowd gathered outside and police had to clear a way through for Fee's mother and sister. Only those with business in the court were admitted, but the crowd remained for most of the day, eager to hear how the case was progressing.

From the prosecution, the jury heard how Fee was the last person seen with John Flanagan and how he had coldly joined in the search for the missing man when he knew exactly where he was. The court heard that Fee had bought a new spade the same afternoon Flanagan had disappeared. Clones ironmonger James Nicholl testified that Fee had rushed into his shop, picked up a spade and told him, 'Put this down to me,' before hurrying out. The pig-sticker knife was identified as Fee's and several witnesses testified that he had fenced off the dung heap shortly after John Flanagan's disappearance.

The accused man had told Anne Flanagan that her brother would turn up and even offered to buy her a drink to settle her nerves as they searched for him. The court heard that Fee's finances seemed to have improved considerably after Flanagan disappeared. The slaughterhouse had never been very successful, and a week before Flanagan had gone missing Fee had bought some pigs on credit. After 16 April he started paying off debts and buying better-quality animals in cash. Also, a purse found on Fee when he was arrested was identified as John Flanagan's.

The defence could do little to refute this evidence, but tried to suggest that Joseph Fee was the victim of rumours and a campaign to condemn him. The defence called three witnesses to claim they had seen that Fee was absent from Clones between 1pm and 3pm on the day of Flanagan's disappearance, visiting a man outside the town.

Under cross-examination the men's evidence was torn apart. Two of the men could not give a date on which the journey had been made, and the third admitted that he had been convicted of drunkenness thirty-one times and was a relative of Fee's. None of them could give any reason why they had not given evidence at the previous trials, except that they were not called. Fee's mother and sister testified that he had not been about to flee when he was arrested.

Before more witnesses for Fee were called, the defence sought an adjournment, explaining that these witnesses had dined too well. Questioned by the judge, he admitted that they were drunk. After three days, the judge summed up the trial and gave the case over to the jury. After less than an hour's deliberation, they came back and found Joseph Fee guilty of the murder of John Flanagan. Fee turned pale as the verdict was given.

Asked whether he could give any reason why he should not be sentenced to death, Fee replied: 'Well, my Lord, the evidence that has been sworn against me by the Crown is all lies – perjury.

I swear now I am innocent. I am not afraid to meet my death; so long as I am innocent I do not care.' There was a moment of silence when the prisoner concluded his statement, and then the judge addressed Fee directly. 'Joseph Fee, two juries of the County Monaghan, the county in which this crime was committed, were either unwilling or unable to come to a conclusion. A jury of the citizens of Belfast, apart from the county in which you were known and carried on your trade, and in which this crime was committed, were irresistibly impelled by the over-whelming nature of the evidence against you to the one and only conclusion they could come to – that yours was the hand, that, on the 16th of April, 1903, struck down John Flanagan. No honest jury or juror who was determined to do his duty, could have come to any other conclusion.'

The judge was in tears as he sentenced Fee to death. Fee, on the other hand, stood impassively as the sentence was delivered. There would be no reprieve for Joseph Fee. He was executed on 22 December 1904 at Armagh Prison.

The Finisher of the Law

The murder of John MacCrossan by John McLaughlin in Omagh, County Tyrone on 27 August 1864 caused a sensation. Demand for reports of the trial was so high that the *Tyrone Constitution* had to reprint the editions containing its accounts several times in the week that followed.

The murder came about as a result of a minor dispute between John McLaughlin and his neighbour Peter Doyle, concerning a wall separating their properties on Castle Street. Both men were carriage-makers and rivals in business. When they went to court over the matter, MacCrossan represented Doyle. The judgement went against McLaughlin and Doyle was awarded damages of £8 plus costs. When McLaughlin failed to pay, the court made an order against him for the amount of the verdict and costs – £56 14s. 6d. – and directed that goods worth that amount be seized from him.

MacCrossan asked his brother Charles, who was sub-sheriff for the county, to execute the order against McLaughlin. On 27 August, Charles went to McLaughlin's house on Castle Street where he found McLaughlin standing at the gate to his yard, and told him he hoped to make the performance of his duty as agreeable as possible under the circumstances. The pair spoke for a while, McLaughlin became enraged, and they exchanged angry words. Eventually McLaughlin ended the discussion by pushing Charles out of the yard and closing the gate.

McLaughlin appeared at an open window above his front door holding an iron bar with a cleek or hook on one end. Charles remonstrated with him. 'Surely you would not use that weapon against me,' he said. McLaughlin told him to go away, and Charles prudently took a few steps back. As he was talking with McLaughlin, his brother John arrived and asked, 'What is this all about?' It was raining and, as he talked to his brother, John was standing under an umbrella beneath McLaughlin's window. Charles cautioned him to move away from the building, but it was too late. McLaughlin drove the iron bar through the umbrella and into the left side of John's neck. Blood gushing from the terrible wound, John was carried home and lingered for nearly a day and a half before passing away.

Ladies and gentlemen, rich and poor of every description, packed the courthouse on 17 March 1865 for the eagerly awaited trial. The first witness for the prosecution was Charles MacCrossan. He recalled arriving at McLaughlin's house to serve the writ and asking him, 'Can nothing be done?' McLaughlin replied that he could do nothing. 'Perhaps, it's not too late yet,' Charles responded. 'I'll try even yet and make some arrangement.'

McLaughlin refused to go with Charles to talk with his brother. 'He's a bad man and would do nothing for me,' McLaughlin said. 'I might expect a favour from you, but not from him.' McLaughlin wanted Charles to go with him to a public house to see if a friend there might lend him the money, but Charles refused to depart the premises without leaving someone in charge, reminding McLaughlin that he intended to seize goods to the value of the writ. McLaughlin made no reply but walked away for a short while, before returning, angrily pushing MacCrossan out into the street, and bolting the gate.

Seeing McLaughlin at the window, Charles tried to persuade him to let him in, but McLaughlin would not listen, threatening him with the iron bar, and giving him 'four minutes to get away'. A servant arrived and Charles sent him to his brother's office to tell him that McLaughlin was not cooperating. Charles did not see his brother arrive until he spoke to him. As he warned John about his safety and tried to lead him away, Charles felt a sudden jerk and tried to support his brother. He saw the iron bar pass close to his own face and blood began to flow. John cried out that he was murdered, and Charles saw 'McLaughlin put out his head and smile down at the people below'.

Several prosecution witnesses testified to seeing McLaughlin hook John MacCrossan with the iron bar. Constable Archibald McCaughan described climbing into McLaughlin's house through the window and arresting him. Searching McLaughlin, he found a small sum of money and a letter from John MacCrossan dated that day and headed 'Doyle v. Yourself.' It read:

Sir, I informed you after the verdict that I had no desire to put you to inconvenience in paying the amount of damages and costs in this cause, and that I would take it from you in such instalments as you could easily pay. I confess I have been rather disappointed that up to the present time you have not offered to pay one penny, and the matter is made worse when I find you engaged in the same reckless lawlessness for which Mr Doyle had to bring the action against you. Please come to my office that we may arrange how you are to pay the amount of the verdict, and bring what money you have with you.

When he took McLaughlin to the lock-up, Constable McCaughan continued, they passed John MacCrossan's house. As they did so McLaughlin said, 'The robbing rascal, it was not enough to take away all my money, but he would take away my wife.' William Doherty, a drummer in the Tyrone militia, testified that McLaughlin had told him on 'August 27th last that he was going to have a dispute about an old wall with Doyle and asked would I see him beaten. I said I would not. He then showed me a cleek he had behind the gate, which he said was "the finisher of the law".'

Cross-examined by the defence, Doherty admitted that he had gone to a public house with the defendant and had drunk some cordial, but he said he had not been drunk. Bernard Stars, McLaughlin's apprentice, told the court he had given Mrs McLaughlin a note he had got from John MacCrossan, and that he had seen his master make two cleeks in his forge. John Maguire, a carpenter who worked there, corroborated this, adding that McLaughlin had told him one was for hooking salmon out of a river and the other was for pulling flax out of a dam.

Medical testimony concerning John MacCrossan's injuries was given by Dr Henry Thompson, who had attended the wounded man shortly after the attack. He told the court there was a small deep cut on the left side of the neck caused by the weapon. The iron bar had injured the base of the skull, causing injury to the brain, which was the cause of death. 'The symptoms of injury to the brain set in on the following day, and I intimated to Mr MacCrossan's friends that we had no hope of him,' Dr Thompson concluded.

The defence counsel told the jury that there was no evidence the attack was a premeditated murder – at worst it was manslaughter. The defence described the iron bar with a hook on the end of it as 'the most awkward instrument which any man of common-sense could make for the purpose of murder'. Besides, if that had been his intention, why did he make two? Did he want to commit two murders? It was far more reasonable to assume that McLaughlin had made the bars for the reasons he had stated.

He had a large field of flax and the hooked bars were suited for pulling flax out of holes. The defence counsel asked if the jury could believe the evidence of a drunken militiaman that the defendant had placed one of the bars at a gateway in daylight for the purpose of committing a murder? When John MacCrossan was struck his head was covered by an umbrella so how would it have been possible for McLaughlin to see where he was lunging with the iron bar? If he had been trying to kill MacCrossan why did he let go of the bar as soon as it touched MacCrossan?

McLaughlin was horrified by what had happened, his defence claimed, and became unhinged in the immediate aftermath of the incident as could be shown by his remarks while passing the injured man's house in the constable's custody. The defence warned the jury not to be taken in by the prosecution's flimsy attempts to prove that the tragedy was wilful murder instead of manslaughter and quoted legal texts explaining the difference.

Several well-respected members of the community gave character references for John McLaughlin. An Omagh magistrate told the court he had known McLaughlin for several years and described him as 'the most peaceable, industrious tradesman in the town'. Three Omagh clergymen of different faiths also testified that he was of good character. One added that he was 'quiet, honest, and hardworking'.

The prosecution's closing address told the jury that if the prisoner had intended only to injure John MacCrossan but had killed him in the process the crime was still murder. In his summing up, the judge suggested that Constable McCaughan had misheard what McLaughlin had said while passing the victim's house, and that it was fair to assume the accused had said MacCrossan had wanted to take away his life, not his wife.

After two and a half hours of deliberation the jury returned a verdict of guilty, but recommended mercy as there was no proof that McLaughlin intended to kill. They believed he had only intended to inflict injury. McLaughlin was stunned. He had only expected to be convicted of manslaughter and jailed for a few months – a year at most. The judged agreed with the verdict and agreed to seek mercy for the guilty man.

When asked if he had anything to say before he was sentenced, McLaughlin replied, 'I was so much agitated, I was not in a state of mind to know what I was doing.' Then, pointing at Charles MacCrossan, he said, 'There is the man that brought it on both of us. He is the murderer of us both!' McLaughlin was sentenced to death, but his case was reviewed a few weeks later and his sentence was commuted to life imprisonment.

A Shot in the Night

Leo Gerrard from Drogheda married Alice Scott in 1941. After the wedding they moved into her widowed mother's house in Donaghmore village near Navan, County Meath. Gerrard worked in England and his trips home to Ireland were infrequent due to the war. When Alice gave birth to a son in May 1946 it was clear that her husband was not the father, as he had not been home nine months before. When Gerrard found out she had given birth to another man's son they had a heated argument and he left Alice in no doubt that he was finished with her. Alice remained with her mother and they got by as best they could.

Alice went to bed at 11.30pm on the night of 5 October 1946. After midnight her mother entered the room with a lit lamp and placed it on the washstand near the bedroom window, which had been left open two inches. Her daughter was fast asleep in the bed she shared with her baby. Mrs Scott then went to bed herself, but she was woken sometime later by the baby crying. She called out, but Alice did not reply, and the baby stopped crying.

Then Mrs Scott heard what she thought was the sound of 'someone walking in stockinged feet'. The baby began crying again and she went into Alice's room to see what was wrong. The lamp had gone out, and Mrs Scott found her way in the dark to the bed. She touched her daughter's head and felt something wet. She fetched a match, lit the lamp, and found herself in hell. Alice was lying on her right side and her face was covered in blood.

Mrs Scott picked up the crying baby from the bed and ran for help. Her next door neighbour, Mary Rath, was the first person to arrive, at about 1.30am. More neighbours soon came to help too. One went for the local priest, and Mary Rath helped tidy Alice's room by dusting the washstand and windowsill. Alice's death was not reported to the gardaí in Navan until 8.30am and it was another two hours before Garda Timothy Cremlin arrived at the house. Alice still lay in her bed and he noted that there were no marks on her head.

At 12pm, Dr Richard Whyte visited the cottage and examined Alice's neck and head and concluded that she had killed herself. When Mrs Rath and two other kindly female neighbours began to lay out the body, they removed Alice's nightdress and discovered a large wound between her right breast and shoulder. The gardaí were called again and arrived an hour later with Dr Whyte, who soon declared that Alice had been shot. The doctor later stated that he had not been happy with his initial diagnosis and had unsuccessfully tried to contact the coroner. Superintendent A.L. O'Neill arrived, ordered the room sealed, and launched a murder investigation.

An autopsy was conducted at Navan mortuary by the state pathologist, Dr John McGrath, who concluded that Alice had died within two minutes of being shot. Neither Mrs Scott nor any of her neighbours had heard a gunshot during the night. Garda James Kavanagh examined the bedroom window and found a small hole at the bottom of a windowpane and noted a corresponding hole – with singed edges – in the lace curtain. The entire window was then removed to Dublin for further technical examination.

Gardaí learned that Alice had a number of lovers and usually left her bedroom window open for them. One of them, John Flood, was eliminated from the list of suspects after witnesses established his whereabouts during the time of the murder. Another, Leo Gerrard, was quickly ruled out as he was in England. Gardaí believed that the murder weapon was a double-barrelled shotgun owned by builder Larry Rogers from Flower Hill in Navan. He kept it in his yard and was known to be careless about securing it. Minute pieces of glass were found in the gun's barrels and in the groove separating them. Scratches on the barrels showed that they had been pushed through the pane before the shot was fired. Marks left by the barrels were found in the putty of the window frame.

One of Alice's lovers, 42-year-old Joseph McManus from Gortoral, County Fermanagh, lived in Rogers' yard, but was nowhere to be found when gardaí went looking for him. On the night of the murder, witnesses had seen him drinking in Navan until closing time. One of the shotgun's cartridges had been found at the murder scene, but a second was missing, so gardaí made a painstaking search to find it. Zooming in on the likely route McManus would have taken back from Alice's home to Flower Hill, two teams of gardaí hunted on their hands and knees for ten days for the missing cartridge. They found four cartridge cases, one of which matched a test cartridge fired from the right barrel of Rogers' shotgun. Particles of glass were found inside the cartridge.

Joseph McManus returned to Rogers' yard on Tuesday, telling a workmate he had been away collecting money owed to him. In his absence, gardaí had searched his caravan and found two minute particles of glass on his bedcover and four more on a bedside bench. Gardaí took McManus to Navan police station and he was questioned by veteran murder investigator Detective Superintendent George Lawlor. During the three-hour interview McManus nervously paced the room. He made no confession and was released without charge, but kept under surveillance.

On Wednesday, McManus got drunk and jumped off a bridge in Navan into the River Boyne. An off-duty garda jumped into to rescue him, but was swept away. Luckily, both men managed to grab tree branches and were rescued. Tests proved that the glass found in the shotgun's barrels and McManus's bed matched the glass from Alice's window, and he was charged with her murder just over a week later.

While McManus was being held in Mountjoy Prison he claimed 'little men' were visiting him in his cell. He was twice found unfit to plead when he was brought before the Central Criminal Court in Dublin, but was declared sane on 4 January 1947 by Dr John Dunne of Grangegorman Mental Hospital and his trial commenced ten days later. McManus pleaded not guilty and the case commenced.

The court heard testimony detailing Alice Gerrard's relationship with McManus and the technical evidence linking him to the crime, as well as the fact that he had borrowed a pair of black dancing shoes from Larry Rogers, which were seen under his bed the day before the murder and later found discarded in a field between his caravan and Alice's home on the route he was known to take.

The defence tried to muddy the case by asking if the jury might consider it strange that McManus had not fled Navan after the murder if he was the killer, and pointing out that he was not the only person with access to the shotgun, and that anyone could have accessed his caravan. In his summing up, the judge told the jury they should consider that the killer would have chosen to wear a pair of light shoes rather than heavy boots to remain silent, and he reminded them of the pair McManus had borrowed before the shooting, which had been found in a field between his caravan and the victim's home.

On 30 January 1947, after four hours' deliberation, the jury found McManus guilty of Alice Gerrard's murder. His appeal was dismissed and he was executed on 31 March 1947.

After his death it was revealed that Alice Gerrard was probably not his first victim. Although the trial jury had not known this, McManus had been the chief suspect for the murder of 20-year-old Martha Lunny in 1923. She had been found raped and beaten to death on 29 March 1923 in a Fermanagh field, just inside Ulster. An autopsy showed that she had died fighting to defend herself from her attacker.

The Lunny family had a business in Swanlinbar in the Free State and Martha routinely walked to the family home in Kinawley in Ulster. The murder investigation was conducted by the RUC and made little headway as locals suspected that she had been killed as a spy and were too frightened to come forward. One exception was 17-year-old local boy Joseph McManus, who eagerly told police that he had met Martha as he crossed the border going south and had seen her attacked by two soldiers from the Free State Army.

McManus was kept in protective custody for six weeks for his own safety. Although he claimed he could identify the men, he could only remember the buttons on their uniforms. Garda detectives investigating the brutal murder came to believe that Martha had known her killer, and they felt that McManus was a likely suspect. By the time they asked the RUC to hold him though, McManus was no longer in custody and had joined the British Army. Stationed in India for several years, he remained in the army until 1935. Martha's murder remained unsolved.

Detective Sergeant Lawlor believed that McManus was guilty of both murders. In his notes on Alice Gerrard's murder, he remarked, 'On his own admission, McManus was present when Martha Lunny was killed, and many people were convinced he was a murderer. In each case, a defenceless female was done to death at night, by a killer who left public roads and went panther-like through the fields after his prey.' One mystery remains. Why did nobody hear the gunshot that killed poor Alice Gerrard?

The Cake of Death

Agnes McAdam lived with her brother Patrick and his wife Tessie on their small farm near Ballybay, County Monaghan. She was 52 years old and unmarried. She had had an accident with a threshing machine some years before and wore a glove over her injured left hand. The accident also had lasting effects on her temperament – she was considered to be a 'nervous woman'. The family lived in a tightknit community and were on good terms with their neighbours.

A short distance away lived the Finnegan family: 65-year-old James, his wife Mary and their daughter Lily. In September 1945, Lily and her friend Kathleen Coyle were put in charge of organising a party for two local priests who were leaving to go abroad to the missions. Over 500 people were expected to attend, and the pair began to collect donations of food and money to hold the function.

On 13 September Lily and Kathleen called to the McAdam household to see if Agnes would bake a cake. Tessie answered the door and told them that Agnes was in bed, but she would pass on the message. Agnes told Tessie she did not think she would bake a cake, as the ingredients were hard to get. When Lily and Kathleen returned four days later, the McAdams donated £1. Agnes was not to be seen and there was no word on whether she would bake a cake.

On the morning of 22 September Agnes cycled to Ballybay and bought two jam sandwich cakes in Smith's bakery in the town. One was a Scribona, wrapped in greaseproof paper inside a cardboard box. The other was made by Lyons of Drogheda. On the way home Agnes cycled past the Finnegan farmhouse, but did not stop to deliver the cakes. Instead, she went home and hung them in a bag on a nail in her bedroom. It was six days before she finally delivered the cakes. She gave them to Mrs Finnegan and told her they 'were just out of the oven' as she was just after cooking them.

Agnes was still there when Lily and her father returned home, but left before the family sat down to have their dinner at 3.30pm. Lily wanted Agnes to write her name on the two cakes so people would know of her generosity, but Agnes refused to do so. After a hearty dinner of herrings, potatoes and milk, James suggested that they should eat one of the cakes intended for the party as there were so many. Lily and Mary agreed.

He took down the smaller of Agnes's cakes and cut it into slices to have with their tea. He had a large piece and gave smaller ones to his wife and daughter. Lily took a mouthful and spat it out almost immediately as it tasted bitter. Her mother noticed the same bitter taste, but ate it anyway. James had the remainder of the cake, with the exception of a piece that fell on the floor.

After tea, James Finnegan said, 'Thank God for a good dinner,' and set off to the bog with his donkey and cart to collect a load of turf. Mary then made a meal up for the family dog and let it into the kitchen to eat. The dog ate the cake that Lily had spat out and the piece that had fallen, and it became very ill. The poor creature began to shiver and foam at the mouth. It was dead within minutes.

Later in the afternoon Mary became very ill. Her limbs became paralysed and she went blind. 'I held onto the walls, and then got outside, when I was vomiting for about an hour,' she said. She was sitting on a stool in the yard when her husband returned home from the bog at 6pm. He staggered through the gate with his teeth gritted but could not reach the house and collapsed in the yard.

James suffered several convulsions and his face turned blue. Neighbours were called, and Lily did her best to help her parents by giving them salt and water to drink. While her mother downed hers and vomited, James was unable even to swallow. Two young women called in to help who were nurses in England, on holidays back home. They gave him baking soda and water, but it did not help him vomit. One of the priests for whom the party was to have been held administered the last rites, and James Finnegan passed away at 7.15pm, before a doctor arrived. Poisoning was immediately suspected, and Lily gave gardaí the other cake from Agnes to be tested.

On 30 September, the day the party was to have been held, Dr John McGrath, the state pathologist, carried out post-mortem examinations on the bodies of James Finnegan and the family dog. He examined the organs and found the deadly poison strychnine. James had consumed more than one grain of strychnine – four times the amount required to kill a person. The other cake from Agnes was found to contain more than half a grain of strychnine.

Gardaí called to the McAdam house and interviewed Agnes. During the three hours they questioned her, she was quite composed, smoking cigarettes and answering intelligently. She told them in detail how she had bought the cakes after hearing that anyone who presented anything would be invited to the party. She had hung them in a bag on a nail in her bedroom and had not even opened the parcel or looked at them before presenting them to Mary Finnegan. 'I gave it as I got it in the shop,' she told the gardaí. Agnes denied having claimed the cakes were homemade and 'just out of the oven'.

She also denied ever buying or owning strychnine. Gardaí then produced a poison register with her signature. It clearly stated she had bought 16 grains of strychnine from Manley's chemist in Ballybay on 16 June 1942 for rats. Agnes denied it. 'I never put my name in that book. No, I did not. That name Agnes McAdam, was never wrote by me ... I never saw all that before.' When asked if it was her writing, Agnes stared at the entry for six minutes before answering, 'I do think I bought that strychnine. I can't remember yet whether or not I bought it. If I did buy that stuff, and if it was got for the rats, it would be given to rats.'

A sergeant recorded the questions and answers from the interview and read the statement back to Agnes. She made no alterations and signed it. Gardaí charged Agnes McAdam with the murder of James Finnegan a few days later. The trial began on 11 February 1946 in the Central Criminal Court in Dublin before Mr Justice Gavan Duffy. She pleaded not guilty and the trial lasted for five days, with evidence from 46 people.

For the prosecution Séan Hooper outlined the case, saying that the defendant had intended to injure or kill somebody by placing poison in the cakes. The main witnesses for the prosecution were Mary and Lily Finnegan. Their chilling testimony was heard first. Dr McGrath gave evidence that

James Finnegan's death was consistent with strychnine poisoning.

For the defence Charles Casey told the jury the prosecution could only present the case as 'one devoid of motive'. He insisted that the crime was the act of a lunatic, as only a mad person would take the life of another without any motive or reason. Agnes McAdam took the stand and told the court she had bought the strychnine in 1942 and mixed it up with mash in order to kill rats and they had eaten it all. When Agnes was asked why she had told gardaí she had never bought or used strychnine Agnes said she had forgotten about it. She concluded her testimony by stating that she had no enmity towards the Finnegans, and, so far as she knew they had none towards her.

Summing up the case the judge reminded the jury that 'society must try as a murderer any person who intentionally created a new hazard of death by handing out a deadly poison for someone in a small community to consume.' Therefore the prisoner was guilty if she knowingly gave Mary Finnegan cakes she knew contained strychnine. If the jury was satisfied that 'she gave the cake with murderous intention the motive did not matter'. The jury returned its verdict after two hours and ten minutes, finding her guilty but strongly recommending mercy.

When asked if she had anything to say about why she should not be sentenced to death, Agnes McAdam quietly replied, 'Not guilty.' Mr Justice Duffy sentenced her to death without putting on the traditional black cap and fixed her execution for the following month. Agnes had to be helped from the dock by two warders.

Although Agnes McAdam's appeal was refused, the government commuted her sentence to life in prison a few days before her execution date. Agnes spent three years in prison before being released in September 1949 to the care of a convent in Wexford, where she remained until she was transferred to the county nursing home thirteen years later. She died in 1963.

Yankee Lynch and the Dark Boy

Ireland once hanged a blind man for murder. Although there was no doubt about his guilt, it took three trials before he was convicted.

The victim was Patrick Lynch from Lackenmore, Ballyjamesduff, County Cavan. Lynch, his wife Rose and their 8-year-old son lived in .comfortable circumstances. He had spent several years working in America and his earnings made life easier for the family. He occasionally returned to America to work for a spell, and he was known to all as 'Yankee' Lynch. His wife had brought a bog worth £10 to the marriage and a dispute over the ownership of this wretched piece of land ultimately led to his death in tragic circumstances.

Lynch's killer was Laurence Smith, who was unmarried and lived with his two brothers and a sister-in-law on their farm nearby. The two men had a lot in common as Smith too had travelled to seek his fortune. He had gone to Australia and worked in diggings during the gold rush before losing his eyesight in an accident and returning home to the family farm. He was known locally as the 'Dark Boy' due to his blindness, and he was a familiar figure in the area, finding his way around with the aid of a stick and a trained dog.

The Smith family strongly believed that the bog was theirs by right, no matter what title Patrick Lynch or his wife held. The feud turned bitter in 1868, when Laurence Smith brought a trespass action against Lynch in relation to the disputed parcel of bog. Smith lost the case and the court awarded costs to Lynch, who refused to pay them.

In September 1869, the Smith family were forced to sell part of their farm to meet the costs of their failed legal case. The land was sold at public auction and fetched £25. The loss of part of their farm was humiliating enough, but the Smith family were enraged when 'Yankee' Lynch purchased it. They refused to surrender possession of the lands to Lynch, and he was forced to take legal proceedings against them. The dispute turned violent in April 1872, when Lynch was beaten on his way home from Ballyjamesduff one night.

Lynch's case against Smith for the court costs was due to be heard in July 1872, and notice of the trial date had been served on the day of Lynch's death. On the morning of 3 July, Lynch went into Ballyjamesduff on business, and he set out for his home again in the early afternoon drunk. Laurence Smith was also in the town, but he remained there for another half hour after Lynch's departure and set out for home by a longer route so he could avoid meeting Lynch. Unfortunately, he overtook the drunken man, an argument ensued, and Smith stabbed Lynch to death.

The murder happened around 3pm on a public road. Several witnesses saw the tragedy unfold and attempted to break up the fight. Lynch is said to have tried to get up from the ground and said, 'See what you have done?' to Smith, and then dropped dead. When news of the murder reached police in Ballyjamesduff, they went straight to the Smith farm and arrested the three brothers. Laurence Smith stepped forward. 'It was I who was in contact with Lynch,' he said.

'You have no business to take them. Don't take them from their families.' When police were satisfied that Laurence Smith's two brothers had played no part in the killing, they were released. Laurence Smith remained in custody.

'I don't consider myself an assassin,' he told Inspector Ware. 'What I did, I did it in my own defence. I look upon myself as a soldier defending himself … Lynch drew the knife first,' he said, and demonstrated how he had taken the knife from Lynch, sliding his hand down Ware's arm until he reached his hand and grabbing an imaginary knife from his grip.

'It was a curious thing you knew this man,' Inspector Ware noted.

'I knew him from his step,' replied Smith. 'When providence takes away one sense, it strengthens the other senses.'

An autopsy showed that Patrick Lynch had been stabbed eighteen times in the chest with a knife. A single-bladed knife, similar to one Smith had bought in Ballyjamesduff sometime before, was found near the crime scene, hidden in a tree stump, covered with moss.

At the first trial, the jury could not agree on a verdict. The prosecution admitted that their case was weak. How could a blind man overtake and kill a sighted man? They could not prove Smith had not been acting in self-defence, as no one knew what exactly had occurred between the deceased and the accused. The jury was told they could bring in a verdict of manslaughter if they believed Smith's evidence.

At the second trial, the jury also failed to agree a verdict. The third trial saw Laurence Smith declared guilty of the murder of Patrick Lynch, but recommended mercy be shown to him. The judge agreed with the verdict and the jury's recommendation, but had no choice but to pass the sentence of death.

The judge later wrote to the lord lieutenant of Ireland to seek a reprieve for Smith, pointing out that Smith and Lynch had met by accident and the crime was not premeditated. Even though there was ill-will between the men, Smith may not have intended to kill Lynch. The judge added that it was without precedent that a blind man should be hanged, no matter what he had been convicted off.

There would be no reprieve. Laurence Smith was hanged at Cavan Gaol on 16 August 1873. The hangman botched the execution – the rope was too long. When the trapdoor was sprung, the condemned man fell with a heavy thud. Instead of instantly breaking his neck, Smith dangled in agony for a minute with his toes slightly touching the ground, until one of the clergymen present ordered the hangman to pull up the rope. He hauled the unfortunate man up a few feet from the ground and left him there until he choked to death. It was a terrible way to die.

Death by Bread

Hannah Loughridge died in agony on 5 August 1823 after eating some bread her husband had given her, which her mother-in-law had made that day. At her funeral two days later, mourners whispered their belief that she had been poisoned, and suspected her husband. It was widely known that their marriage had not been a happy one.

Hugh Loughridge lived at Polintamny, County Antrim, a few miles away from Ballymoney. He was 28 years old and blind. Despite this disability, he rented a small farm and did as much work as a blind person was able to. He had married Hannah Houston a few years before. They had two young children, and they constantly quarrelled. Hugh's elderly parents lived next door and his 75-year-old mother Esther was on bad terms with Hannah.

Mother and son were arrested a few days after Hannah's death and charged with her murder. They were imprisoned in Carrickfergus Gaol while awaiting trial. Usually such proceedings took place a few weeks after an arrest, but for some reason the Loughridges were not brought to trial until 12 August 1824, a year later.

The first prosecution witness was the Loughridges' 14-year-old servant girl, Sarah Evans, who testified that the couple were not on good terms. Relating the events of 5

August, Sarah told the court that she had spent the day with Hannah on the bog, footing turf. They returned home that evening and while she went out to gather a basket of potatoes for their supper, Hannah rested in the kitchen. When Sarah returned, Hannah had a piece of buttered oaten bread. Hannah took a few bites, said it had a bad taste, and refused to eat anymore. Hugh and Esther were also in the kitchen.

Hugh said she need not complain as they had eaten the same bread before she came home. Esther left for her own house. Hannah asked Sarah to fetch her a drink of water and she took it. She went to spin yarn, but soon afterwards returned to sit at the fire, saying she wished she had not eaten the bread, for her 'heart was burning'. Esther returned a short while later and Hugh told her: 'Hannah blames the bread you gave her, for making her bad.' Esther angrily replied 'that was the thanks people got for giving their kindness'. Hannah responded that 'if it had been for her good she would not have got it,' adding that 'they had often striven for her life, and they had gotten it at last'.

Hannah then lay down in bed, her condition worsened, and she vomited again and again until she died. All along, she repeatedly asserted that her husband and mother-in-law had poisoned her. Under cross-examination, Sarah said Hannah had been perfectly heathy until she had eaten the bread. She ate nothing else, haven taken ill before dinner was ready, and went to bed half an hour later. Hannah had been nursing a 20-week-old infant and her sister-in-law had given the child some milk. During the time she was ill Hannah refused to speak to her husband. She knew she was dying.

A neighbour, Margaret McLister, told the court she had heard Hannah was ill and went to see her. She found her friend 'very ill and moaning'. Hannah's eyes were shut, but she knew Margaret and told her, 'I will not be long with you now.' Hannah drank a little water and said that 'her heart was burning'. Margaret had to go milk her three cows, and by the time she returned Hannah was dead. She had died with her mouth open and Margaret could not get it shut. Margaret testified that she was 'greatly surprised to find froth at the mouth, and water running from the mouth and nose'. Hannah's sister Jane Houston told the court she arrived six or seven hours after her sister had died and found the 'corpse was dark and had four black spots on the side of the neck; froth was at her mouth, and water proceeded from her nose and mouth in great quantities'.

The court heard from Jane Johnston of Ballymoney, the wife of the local surgeon, that she had sold Hugh Loughridge three-quarters of an ounce of white arsenic on 2 August 1823, for the purpose of killing rats. She had kept a record of the sale. Twelve-year-old Robert Irwin testified that he had taken the blind man to Johnston's shop and had witnessed him buy three pence worth of the poison. He had been told it was to kill rats, who were 'destroying his butter'.

Robert's father John Irwin testified that Hugh Loughridge had told him he had bought the poison for 'Mr Brice of the Knockagh', to kill vermin. Loughridge had told him his wife was 'donsy or a little tender'. Irwin asked if she was 'confined' and was told that she was in the turf bog. Loughridge told Irwin that 'it run in his mind she would not be long to the forer, and that, when she died, he would send for her relations and give her a decent funeral'. He told Irwin he had a piece of cloth for a gown, which he said was for his servant girl and asked Irwin to keep it as 'there was a little jealousy' between his wife and the girl. A few days later John Irwin heard that Hannah, who was a relation of his, was dead.

Carrickfergus prison doctor John McGowan testified from the evidence heard in court that the symptoms seemed to be the same as those produced by 'acrid poison or arsenic'. He added that the symptoms might also arise from other causes.

When Hannah's father William Houston testified, he was visibly upset. There had been no inquest he said, and no doctor had examined the corpse. He could not imagine that his daughter had been poisoned, although it had been rumoured at the funeral. Houston could not believe Hugh Loughridge 'could be so barbarous'.

The judged summed up the case, showing where the evidence might support the charge of murder and where it might be favourable towards the accused. He then gave the case to the jury. Without leaving the court, the jury returned their verdict, finding both mother and son guilty of the murder of Hannah Loughridge. When the two were asked why they should not be sentenced to death, Hugh spoke first, in a 'firm tone of voice'.

'I have to say, my Lord, I am not guilty,' he said. 'By the reason, that when I went to Ballymoney for the arsenic, it was for Mr Brice, and on my return I gave it to his servant, as I considered. When I was charged with the murder of my wife, I went to Mr Brice, but he denied having received the poison, desiring me to point out the person I had given it to, but I told him I could not, because I was blind. The girl makes evidence that she returned from the bog with the deceased. This is wrong, for if she had been present she would have seen I ate as much of the bread as the deceased.

We shall submit to any judgment passed on us, but we are wrongly accused by these people, and are not guilty.'

Esther Loughridge asserted her innocence, saying she knew nothing of the poison. A newspaper account describes her as a 'hoary woman, upwards of sixty years old', and said she did not 'evince much feeling on the awful occasion'.

The judge, visibly affected, then addressed the prisoners. All present in court were deeply moved as he pronounced the dreadful sentence of death and told them that they would be hanged in three days' time.

The next day, Esther gave the prison matron ten pence, which she had earned in prison by spinning, and asked her to take it to her son so he could pay back money he had borrowed in prison. The matron gave the money to Hugh and told him that if his mother was innocent and he was guilty he ought to confess as it was probably the only way of saving her life.

After a few moments consideration Hugh asked to see Rev. Reid. He confessed that he had poisoned his wife as they 'had always lived on bad terms'. He had bought the poison on 2 August and kept it in his pocket until 5 August. After his wife and Sarah had gone to the bog, he had told his mother there was no bread and his wife would be hungry when she came home. He had asked his mother to bake a loaf and gave her a bowl of meal mixed with the arsenic to do so. She had had no idea there was poison in it.

When the mixture was ready, Hugh had cooked it at the fire and buried the remaining mixture in the bowl outside. He had buttered a piece and given it to his wife on her return. He had also eaten a little. 'It pained me a good deal afterwards,' he admitted. He had buried the rest of the bread outside, including the buttered piece his wife had not finished. Rev. Reid presented Loughridge's confession to the judge who had tried the case, but he refused to commute Esther's sentence, saying he was satisfied of the guilt of both parties.

Hugh and Esther spent their remaining time in prayer and were attended by Rev. Reid and another clergyman. They slept well the night before their execution and had a hearty breakfast that morning. They were due to be executed by the hangman's wife, as he was in Derry seeing to another hanging, but the woman took ill at 10am on execution day. Three other prisoners volunteered and one was picked to carry out the hanging in exchange for a lighter sentence.

Before 1pm, Hugh was pinioned in his cell after stripping off his coat, shoes, and stockings. Wearing a waistcoat and trousers that were 'exceedingly shabby', he was conducted to the execution platform. His elderly mother, bent with age, was helped up the stairs to the platform and both were seated on chairs placed opposite the trapdoor. Nearly two thousand people had gathered outside the prison to witness the execution. Having inquired if any of his friends were present, Hugh was told there was 'not a soul belonging to him there'.

At this he sighed deeply, but said nothing. Esther was agitated and fearful. Although she had not seen her son since the trial, she did not show any emotion towards him or speak to him. Rev. Reid stood before them and asked if they had anything further to say than what they had already admitted, before they appeared in front of God. Hugh admitted his guilt but declared that his mother was innocent of all knowledge of the crime. Esther said she was innocent of the charge.

HIS SIGHTLESS EYES ROAMING UNSTEADILY ABOUT.

Esther and Hugh Loughridge are executed together.

When Rev. Reid asked if she forgave her son, Esther hesitated and then said she did.

'O Hughey,' Esther added. 'If you had told me what was your intention. I would have endeavoured to persuade you from it.'

'It is over now,' Hugh replied.

Rev. Reid gave out Psalm 23, which the Loughridges wished sung, and they both joined in the singing. Then the clergyman read from the twentieth verse to the end of the fifteenth chapter of 1 Corinthians. He prayed with them then took his leave.

The executioner advanced to do his duty, putting black caps on the Loughridges' heads and tightening the cords that bound their arms. Hugh said nothing, but Esther exclaimed, 'Eh, dear me, surely that's the hardest tying that was ever tied.' The ropes were then put about their necks, and hearing the windlass adjusting them to the proper length, the old woman looked around to see what the noise was. The pair did not shed a tear or shake hands throughout. They only prayed.

The Loughridges were then conducted onto the trapdoor, and Hugh said in a firm voice that he hoped his fate would be a warning to all that day. The caps were then drawn over their faces and a cord was lightly tied around the old woman's dress for decency. They were launched into eternity without any signal and Esther died instantly. Hugh struggled for several minutes. After hanging for forty minutes, the bodies were lowered into the street, put into coffins, and then sent off under guard to the county infirmary at Lisburn for dissection. The hangman's wife died later that day.

The Handkerchief

One particular murder case is notable for the great lengths to which the murderer went to avoid suspicion. He was a farmer named Michael McGuinness from near Claremorris, County Mayo. McGuinness was a very tall man for his time, standing nearly six feet, and he was very well built and strong. In 1830, he lived with his elderly mother Margaret and his wife Mary, a young woman, whom he had not been married to long. By all accounts they had a happy marriage and neighbours never had any reason to think otherwise, though Mary's brothers would later say differently.

One evening when McGuinness had gone to the market in Claremorris, his mother, who was described as a 'withered hag, bent with age', hobbled in terror to the nearest cabin and alarmed her neighbours by saying that she had heard a noise in the house and feared that her daughter-in-law was doing harm to herself in her bedroom. Some of the neighbours quickly went to the McGuinness house and discovered the lifeless naked body of the unfortunate young woman lying on a heap of potatoes.

There was no mark of violence on any part of her body except her throat, round which a handkerchief was suffocatingly tied. Blood was pouring from her ears. The poor woman had clearly been strangled – her neck and head were swollen and blackened. According to the old woman her son had not yet returned from the market, and she herself would not have had the strength needed to strangle Mary, even if she had wanted to. While the old woman was callously playing her part, her son, who had not yet been seen to have returned from the market, was arranging his elaborate alibi.

McGuinness had sneaked back home, murdered his wife, and then fled the scene without being spotted by anyone. After crossing a nearby river, he happened to meet a tailor who travelled from one village to another to ply his craft – someone he presumably knew. On the spur of the moment, McGuinness rashly set a plan in motion to try and deflect suspicion for his wife's murder away from himself.

He seized the tailor and forced the man to his knees, making the poor man swear he would never tell anyone what McGuinness was about to reveal to him, and would strictly do as he was told. If he refused, McGuinness promised to 'beat out his brains and fling him into the river'. The terrified tailor swore the oaths McGuinness required, and then he listened in horror to the other man's confession of his wife's murder.

McGuinness then proceeded to make it look like he had been attacked, 'cutting and dinging his hat in several places', and hitting his own face and body repeatedly, leaving cuts and bruises. He ordered the tailor to say he had found the injured McGuinness by the roadside, after he had been attacked by four men on his return from Claremorris. To strengthen the story, he then forced the terrified tailor to carry him on his back to a cabin some distance away, making it look like McGuinness was too weak to walk unaided after the violent assault he had supposedly suffered.

Fearing he would be McGuinness's next victim, the tailor did as he was told. Reaching the cabin, the tailor sought help and told the story he had been directed to tell. The murderer gave an excellent performance as an injured man, relating in a weak voice that he had been attacked by men unknown to him. He pretended to be so feeble that he fainted and fell off his chair.

A common cure for illness at this time was to bleed the patient. Going to great lengths to make his story seem true, McGuinness asked for a local farrier to bleed him. The man – clearly a jack of all trades – did as requested. He closely observed McGuinness, shrewdly noting (according to evidence he gave later) that he did seem weak at all, except for his voice, and that his pulse was strong and regular. The farrier was not the only one to disbelieve McGuinness's claims. The authorities immediately doubted him, and both McGuinness and his mother were committed to jail on suspicion of the murder.

The terrified tailor fled the following day and did not return to the area until the assizes, when he came forward, presumably as much induced by the large reward offered for the murderer's conviction as by the desire to unburden himself of the dreadful secret McGuinness had confessed to him. The trial attracted much interest at the Mayo summer assizes held in August 1830. Mother and son stood jointly accused before Mr Justice Vandeleur of the murder of Mary McGuinness on 24 May.

Mr George French appeared for the prosecution, while Mr Guthrie defended the prisoners. Mr French said he had never come across such an extraordinary murder, even going as far as saying that it reminded him of something from the

'Arabian Nights'. He then stated the case, and called the main prosecution witness, the tailor, whose damning testimony had a stronger ring of truth to it than the murderer's claims.

The deceased woman's brother, Denis Bigley, was called to the witness stand and spoke movingly of his sister. He stated that he had met McGuinness in Claremorris on the day of the murder, but had not spoken to him as they were not on good terms due to McGuinness's mistreatment of his sister. He told the court that McGuinness was a bad husband and often beat Mary, adding that she had been pregnant when she was killed.

Mary's other brother, John, testified that he had drunk a glass of whiskey at the fair with his brother-in-law. Michael McGuinness had pulled out a handkerchief from his pocket at the time. This was the same handkerchief used to kill his sister, and afterwards found round her neck. John Bigley knew the handkerchief well – he had previously given it to his sister as a present.

A Dr Prendergast reported the results of a post-mortem examination of the body. Mary McGuinness's death was clearly caused by strangulation, he said. Dr Prendergast believed that the second knot on the handkerchief could not have been made by the deceased. He also had examined Michael McGuinness, and had found scratches on his head and legs.

Two policemen testified about a conversation McGuinness had with his mother while under arrest in the guard house. They had spoken in Irish, but the policemen had understood. McGuinness had changed his shirt in the guard house. Margaret McGuinness had refused to hand over the shirt Michael had removed when asked to do so. The police took it from under her clothes and found that the sleeve had been partly washed, but there was still blood on it.

The accused had little to base a defence around, and the case was quickly brought to a conclusion. The jury found McGuinness guilty of the murder after an hour's deliberation, and acquitted his mother for want of evidence, much to the displeasure of the people who had crowded into the courtroom.

Mr Justice Vandeleur then passed sentence, condemning McGuinness to death. The sentence was never carried out, as the murderer was found hanged in his cell the next day. He had been hanged by the same handkerchief that he had killed his wife with. McGuinness had fastened the handkerchief to the hinge of the cell door, which was not more than three feet from the ground. How the handkerchief had got into his cell no one would say.

The Accusing Hand

Patrick Doherty was shot twice through the head, once through the heart and once through the wrist. When his father James claimed he had shot himself and then jumped out a window it was clear he had murdered his own son. In any murder case that would be sensational enough. But the most remarkable incident occurred when James and his brother Anthony carried the body into the house after the tragedy.

One of the shots had passed through Patrick's right hand as he held it up in an effort to shield himself. When he died, his arm remained in the raised position. Anthony tried to pull the arm down to a more natural position at the body's side, but rigor mortis had set in and the arm 'slowly rose to its original position, as if denouncing the murderer'. Seeing this, James immediately, 'as if struck with remorse', had an epileptic fit and fell to the floor. Reports of the trial featured in newspapers around the world alongside headlines such as 'Culprit Accused by the Dead Hand' or 'The Accusing Hand'. The bizarre incident was even the subject of a *Ripley's Believe It or Not!* cartoon.

The relationship between father and son had become strained in the months before 27-year-old Patrick's death. The young man lived with his 65-year-old father James in

The corpse points to the killer.

Kilcare, County Leitrim. James ran the village post office and farmed 56 acres. In August 1901 a deed was prepared to transfer the farm to Patrick in exchange for £100. James signed the deed and Patrick witnessed it.

The father, however had second thoughts and made it clear that he did not wish to honour the deed. The pair engaged in a heated argument and the police were called to intervene. When the police arrived they saw James putting his son out of the house, tearing the coat off his back. James told police the deed had been forged and he was going to bring his son to court over it. He did later commence proceedings against Patrick, but did not go ahead with them. Matters were strained further in January 1902, when James complained to the police that his son had interfered with the lock on his shop.

Sergeant Glynn, who was stationed at Keshcarrigan, nearly 3 miles away, inspected the lock but could find no evidence of any interference. At James Doherty's trial, the prosecution claimed this was another imaginary grievance against his son. Soon after the accusation about the lock, Patrick told Sergeant Glynn his father had tried to injure him with an iron hook.

When Sergeant Glynn questioned James about this incident, the man turned to his son and said, 'I'll fix you at last, my boy!' He began eviction proceedings against his son, but on 14 January the pair reached an agreement: Patrick could stay in the house until May, and would receive £100 to depart afterwards.

Next, James engaged a matchmaker to find himself a wife. A 25-year-old Roscommon woman called Mary Holland, who worked in Carrick-on-Shannon, was interested. The 65-year-old man went as far as to meet the girl's father and try to make a deal with him, promising to sign over his farm to her if she married him in two days' time. In the end, Mary Holland, with her family's blessing, declined to marry James Doherty, as he was too old for her and 'quarrelling in a family would never suit her'.

James was enraged and refused to accept that Mary had acted freely. He told police that Patrick had threatened the Holland family to force them to call off the marriage. He bought a revolver in a hardware shop in Carrick-on-Shannon, telling the owner he would get a licence from Sergeant Glynn, and bring it back to show the shop owner. Five days later, Patrick was killed with this same revolver.

James was charged with his son's murder and faced trial in Leitrim in June 1902. Although it was a clear case of murder in the eyes of many, the jury in this first trial could not reach a verdict. One juror wanted to acquit Doherty, while the others wished to convict him.

A second trial took place in Sligo in December 1902, and the prosecution outlined their case once again. Sergeant Glynn provided testimony detailing events leading up to the murder. He also told the court James had sought a licence from him for a revolver. Glynn had flatly told him that no magistrate would grant him a licence for a revolver, but he could get a shotgun licence in May, once his son had left. He testified that James had told him he was afraid his son was out of his mind, as he often paced his room talking to himself. Sergeant Glynn described Patrick Doherty as a 'very decent, orderly boy'.

Mary Holland's father reiterated his daughter's reasons for refusing to marry Doherty, adding that the family had never met Patrick and had never been threatened by him. A Sergeant Gaffney testified that he had met James on 20 March and had been told Patrick was out late at night and keeping bad company. The owner of the hardware shop, who had sold the revolver and fifty cartridges to Doherty on 17 March, testified that he had said he would get a licence from Sergeant Glynn. Neighbours of Doherty told the court that James Doherty had come to their house at midnight on 22 March and told them 'Pat had shot himself'. They said they had rushed to the scene, and then gone for the police.

Anthony Doherty told the court how he had been woken at 1am on 23 March by his brother telling him, 'Get up! Pat shot himself.' At the farm he had found his nephew lying on the ground outside the house and helped to carry him inside. His brother was very distressed, he added. When questioned about the raised arm by the judge, Anthony said, 'The fit came on my brother when the dead man's arm commenced to rise.'

'This is a very solemn occurrence,' said the judge.

Sergeant Glynn was recalled and testified that he had gone to the house with two constables shortly after news of the suspicious death had reached him and examined the murder scene. In the deceased's bedroom there was a track of blood on the windowsill and the window had been broken out, but a bloodstained lamp and a book were sitting on the windowsill. It would not have been possible for a man to have gone out through the window without knocking these things outside also, Sergeant Glynn said. After he examined the room, he inspected the corpse and noted four bullet wounds: one on each side of the nose, one in the hand, and one in the temple. Under the window he found a turf basket covering blood stains. When Glynn returned to the kitchen, Doherty was sleeping. When he awoke he held his hands over his head and said, 'Oh, Sergeant, what will become of me?'

A post-mortem examination carried out by Dr Delaney the next day showed the extent of the deceased's injuries more clearly than Sergeant Glynn had been able to make out by lamplight. In addition to the two shots to the chest, one in the head and one in the wrist, Doherty's skull had been fractured by a heavy blunt instrument. He noted the dead man would have had to have been dead for two hours before rigor mortis set in. Head Constable Crowe told the court he had arrived at the farm at 2am and inspected the crime scene. He believed it was impossible for the deceased to have gone out of the window head first and must have gone out feet first. Searching the deceased's pockets, he found seven revolver bullets rolled up in paper. The paper was bloodstained but the pocket was clean.

The defence sought to claim there was no motive for James Doherty to kill his son as any dispute between father and son had long since been settled. Why would he kill his son to get him out of the house a few days early? As for the revolver, he would hardly go to the police looking for a licence if he was going to commit a murder. The defence claimed there had been two or more people in the room when Patrick was shot and pointed out that blood had been found everywhere except on James Doherty. As for the epileptic fit, Doherty was known to have fits when excited.

The prosecution summed up their case by asking why James Doherty bought the revolver and fifty cartridges if not to commit murder. Doherty had then spent two hours after the murder trying to conceal his guilt and even planting bloodstained cartridges in the deceased's pockets. It was clear James Doherty had shot his son to death in the yard. When summing up the case, the judge directed the jury to discount any theory of suicide as it was clear the deceased had been murdered. He asked them to consider how cartridges wrapped in bloodstained paper ended up in an otherwise clean pocket.

Was it the same hand who had placed the lamp and book in the window and tried to cover a pool of blood with a basket? Who put the revolver in the bedroom if the deceased had been killed outside? There was no other person but James Doherty who could have put them there. He called the murder a crime against the laws of God and a 'crime against nature – a revolting crime'.

After deliberating for only twenty minutes, the jury brought in a verdict of guilty, but recommended mercy on account of the prisoner's previous good character. When asked if he had anything to say about why the sentence of death should not be passed on him, Doherty replied, 'I am as innocent as the child unborn of the murder, my lord.' The judge advised Doherty to make his peace with God and not to hold out any hope of mercy. He sentenced Doherty to be executed on 30 December 1902.

'My lord, grant me a longer day,' pleaded Doherty, but the judge ordered him to be taken away. No reprieve was granted to James Doherty, and he was executed as scheduled in Sligo Gaol. His last words before being hanged were, 'I offer up my life for that of my son, Lord have mercy on his soul.'

Death before Breakfast

George Nugent Reynolds was murdered by Robert Keon in 1786 after a bitter dispute escalated, with fatal consequences. Keon was a solicitor in Carrick-on-Shannon and Reynolds was a local gentleman. The origins of the dispute are unclear, but it seems most likely that it was due to Reynolds advising his mother to fire Robert Keon as her agent. Aggrieved at the loss of this lucrative income, Keon let it be known that he intended to horsewhip Reynolds. Unfortunately, they met soon afterwards at the Leitrim summer assizes of 1786 at Carrick-on-Shannon and Keon carried out his threat, publicly whipping Reynolds outside the courthouse, where the judges were sitting at the time.

This being the age when disputes often led to duels, convention dictated that Reynolds should issue a challenge as a matter of course. Just why there was a delay between the whipping and Reynolds issuing a challenge is not clear. Reynolds had previously fought a duel and had been lucky enough to escape the encounter unhurt. It had been a close shave – his opponent's pistol ball had gone through Reynolds' hat. It is understandable that he might have tried to avoid another risky encounter.

The duel was arranged for the early morning of 18 October 1786 on the Hill of Sheemore, which lay between

Carrick-on-Shannon and Leitrim. Although convention dictated that the pair duel to satisfy their honour, Reynolds had no interest in bloodshed. The evening before the duel he sent his friend, James Plunkett, to Keon with a request that the pistols be loaded with powder only, in order that the demands of the code of honour be satisfied without any risk to either man. He thought Keon had agreed to this. The next morning Reynolds arrived at the meeting place with Plunkett, unarmed, except for a whip.

They found that Robert Keon and his brothers, Ambrose and Edmond, had arrived before them at the appointed place – and they had come heavily armed. Reynolds wished Robert Keon a 'good morning' and doffed his hat. Keon angrily shouted back words to the effect of, 'You damned scoundrel, why did you bring me here?' Keon raised his pistol, pointed it at Reynolds' forehead and coldly shot him dead. James Plunkett cried out, 'A horrid murder!' Ambrose Keon replied, 'If you don't like it, take that,' and attempted to fire a pistol at him. Luckily, it misfired and Plunkett got away safely.

The murder caused a sensation and Robert was arrested, along with Ambrose and Edmond. The trial was due to be held in Carrick-on-Shannon on 23 March 1787, but only sixteen prospective jurors showed up, which wasn't enough to pick a jury from, and so the case was put back to the next assizes. Seeing that there was good reason to believe the Keons would not face impartial judgment in Leitrim, the Crown decided to move the trial to the court of king's bench in Dublin, 100 miles away. The accused would still face a jury composed of County Leitrim jurors, but the trial would be held away from where local sympathy for the accused was strongest.

Prospective jurors continued to be unwilling to co-operate, so the trial could not be held in June and was put back again to 16 November. This time 242 prospective jurors made the journey to Dublin. By the time the trial was held, the defendants had been imprisoned for thirteen months. Despite this, the defence sought a postponement. The defence declared that there was widespread prejudice against Robert Keon and took issue with the impartiality of the jurors.

They had been poisoned against Keon, who had even been compared to Cain, the defence argued. Popular ballads about the murder had been openly sung on the streets of Dublin and had no doubt inflamed opinions. As a result, the defence requested an adjournment until January to let passions cool and allow for a fair trial. This appeal was rejected on the grounds it would be difficult to bring up so many Leitrim freeholders to Dublin again.

The first day was taken up by legal arguments and picking the jury so the trial proper only began the following morning at 9am. A packed court witnessed the judges enter first. Afterwards, Robert Keon was brought in and placed in the dock. Two soldiers with drawn bayonets guarded the prisoner. The prosecution opened their case by recounting the tragic events, emphasising the agreement between the parties to load the pistols with powder only. As to Robert Keon's motive for acting as he had, it could not be said he acted in the heat of the moment or in self-defence – it could only be concluded that his deep hatred of his victim had caused him to murder George Nugent Reynolds.

The main prosecution witness was James Plunkett, who wept as he gave his evidence. Plunkett related how he had gone to Keon's father's house at Reynolds' request and met Robert and his brothers. On hearing the proposal to load the pistols with powder, Robert and Ambrose had been angry, but Edmond was not averse to the suggestion. Edmond and Plunkett had spoken privately, and they had agreed to load the pistols only with powder. Robert and Ambrose were persuaded to accept the proposal, but remained 'sullen'. Despite this, Plunkett had left the house believing an agreement had been reached. Saying his goodbyes to the brothers, Plunkett had said he was glad they had settled the 'disagreeable business in an amicable manner'. Robert had replied that he would 'settle it as he thought proper'.

James Plunkett then told the court how he, Reynolds and two servants arrived at the appointed place as agreed. His servant carried a case of pistols loaded only with powder. Plunkett had brought two pistol balls in his waistcoat pocket to use should a proper duel be unavoidable. Approaching the spot, they saw the Keons standing on a hill 40 yards from the road. Plunkett jumped his horse over the ditch and headed for the Keons at an easy pace. Reynolds dismounted and gave his horse to his servant to hold. He took off his great coat and left it with his servant, before jumping over the ditch and following Plunkett.

Robert Keon and James Plunkett met as they passed each other and Plunkett remarked that he hoped he would 'behave himself politely'. Keon frostily replied he would 'behave as he pleased'. Plunkett was still advancing towards Edmond and Ambrose when he heard Reynolds greet Keon with a good morning and heard the angry response. At the sound of the pistol he looked around and saw his friend fall to the ground, holding his hat. Robert Keon coldly stood over his victim holding his pistol, showing no regret for what he had done. When Ambrose's pistol misfired, Plunkett went to make for Reynolds, but his servant urged him to flee instead. He grabbed one of the unloaded pistols from his servant, put a bullet in it and fled for his life. The servants corroborated Plunkett's testimony and the prosecution concluded their case.

The defence witnesses tried to claim that there had been no agreement to use only powder and the men had met with the intention of fighting a duel. They claimed that Reynolds' hat fell off leaping the ditch and he had picked it up. They testified he had hit Keon several times with his whip and had hit Keon's hand holding the pistol and it went off accidentally and shot him in the head.

The judge summed up the case for both sides, and asked the jury how likely it was that a man, unarmed except for a whip, would attack an armed man, who also had two armed brothers. He reminded them of the lack of remorse shown by Keon after he had killed Reynolds, and then left the case in their hands. The jury brought back a verdict of guilty after twenty minutes.

Over the next few months Keon made a number of attempts to overturn the verdict, but all of these failed. On 31 January 1788 the death sentence was passed, and the execution was scheduled for 16 February. No sooner had the judge pronounced the sentence than a lady dressed in widow's clothing stood up and said, 'I have fled from my home. I have travelled 100 miles to hear this sentence. The blood of my murdered husband cries to heaven for vengeance, and its cry is heard.'

On the day of his execution, at 12am, Robert Keon stepped onto the gallows accompanied by a clergyman. He was about the address the crowd when he caught sight of Reynolds' widow at the window of a house overlooking the gallows. She stood there looking at him, her arm extended, pointing her finger downwards, 'as if to hell'. The condemned man said nothing, but fell to his knees and waited for death. When the trap was sprung, the drop was not fatal. It took Keon twenty minutes to die in agony as George Nugent Reynolds' widow looked on.

The Best Friend

John Long and William Gambon met as patients in St Kevin's Hospital in Dublin during the early 1940s and became close friends. Shortly afterwards, Long moved to England and found employment as a labourer at a military base in Buckinghamshire. Gambon stayed in Dublin and remained mostly unemployed, but the pair remained in touch and Long sent Gambon amounts ranging from 5 shillings to £1 in weekly letters.

Gambon spent a short spell in prison for theft and was later arrested for vagrancy. He survived on money scrounged from friends like Long. In April 1948 he married Margaret Ahearne and the couple moved into a one-room tenement flat on the ground floor at 5 Upper Abbey Street, just off O'Connell Street.

Long arrived in Dublin for a holiday on Saturday 21 August and the friends arranged to meet. Two days later, Margaret Gambon, who had stayed with her cousin in Cabra while Long was visiting, received a letter from her husband saying he had killed someone. The two women went to the flat, but were unable to get in as it was padlocked. When they looked through the window they saw a form lying on the bed and went straight to the gardaí.

When gardaí forced their way into the flat they discovered a man's body on a bed covered with a bedspread. The man's head was battered and bloody and the corpse had lain there for some time. They also found an empty wallet on the floor and a letter addressed to William Gambon from John Long in England. An iron bar beneath the room's washstand looked clean, but it could have been used to kill the man.

An investigation began and the newspapers of 24 August announced that gardaí were anxious to interview William Gambon, describing him as about 28 years old, thin and sun-tanned with hazel eyes and dark hair that was wavy in front – about five foot six. The following morning Gambon walked into Store Street Garda Station, produced a paper containing a report of the murder and announced that he was the killer. When charged with Long's murder, Gambon said, 'I did not do it deliberately. I did not mean to kill the man at all. I did not at any stage intend to kill John Long. I regarded him as the best friend I ever had.'

Seeking further information about John Long, gardaí made an appeal for anyone who had known him to get in touch. They described him as being five foot six, slightly built, with blue eyes, brown hair, and a long, thin, clean-shaven face. Also, his second finger was missing from his right hand.

Gambon's trial began on 1 November 1948 before Mr Justice Cahir Davitt and lasted for three days. That Gambon was guilty of his friend's murder was never in doubt, as he had voluntarily made a statement confessing to the heinous crime when he had turned himself in. Nonetheless, Gambon pleaded not guilty.

For the prosecution, Mr R. F. McLoughlin said Gambon arranged for his wife to stay away on the night Long arrived from England and remain away in the days afterwards or be unable to enter the flat. It was clear that Gambon and Long spent the early hours of Sunday alone in the room as another tenant heard them talking in the yard at 2.15am and going back inside to Gambon's flat. This was the last time John Long was known to be alive.

The next morning, Gambon went to see his wife in Cabra. Later on, James Nolan, who knew both men, met Gambon at the corner of Upper Abbey Street and Capel Street and spoke to him. Gambon gave Nolan £1 for his wife and the two men went and had breakfast. When Nolan asked if Gambon had heard anything from Long he didn't reply and changed the subject, asking Nolan to get him a padlock. Nolan got a lock with two keys and a chain.

On his arrest, Gambon produced two keys, which fitted the lock, and a wallet containing thirty-nine £1 Bank of England notes and a registered envelope bearing the name John Long. In his statement Gambon detailed how he had played pontoon with Long, who had got into the bed. Long lost £60 to Gambon in the process and was very unhappy about it. He said he did not think it was a fair game and demanded Gambon give him back the money.

'The rest of it is a bit hazy,' he said when he was arrested. 'He started calling me all sorts of names and threatened to get up and kick the guts out of me.' Gambon told him to cool off and not be a child, but this only made matters worse.

'Then he started saying filthy things about my wife. I got mad altogether,' Gambon's statement continued. 'I made a dig at him in the bed and missed him. He tried to get a grip on me by the coat. It was then I saw a bar of the washstand which I used for holding up the window. I took the bar in my hand and pushed him away from me with it, back in the bed, and after that everything went blank. But I'm sure that I hit him once with the bar. When I saw the blood he was lying down in the bed. I was out in the street when I came to my senses and it was not until I was at Cabra Road that I realised what I had done. For the life of me I don't remember how I got to Cabra Road. Then I wanted to go back, but I was afraid I might find I had killed him.'

A clerk from Long's local Buckinghamshire post office gave evidence that he had withdrawn his entire savings of £55 in English bank notes. Sergeant J. Hefferen, who had entered the flat with Sergeant J. Dunlea after forcing the lock on the door, told the court that Long had been wearing his waistcoat under his shirt. A pocket of the waistcoat had been cut. Defence Counsel Mr D. Bell suggested that it would have been have been difficult to remove Long's wallet from the small cut in his waistcoat pocket, but Sergeant Hefferen thought it would have been possible. Sergeant Dunlea testified that there did not appear to have been a struggle in the room.

The court next heard from state pathologist Dr J. McGrath, who testified that Long's head was pressed deeply into the pillow and concluded that the blows were inflicted on it while it was in that position. The wounds could have been inflicted by violent blows with an iron bar found in the room, he said. The pathologist also noted that the end of the bar had been heated. If that had been done after the bar had been used, it would have removed the bloodstains from it. Dr McGrath told the court there were four wounds on Long's head, any of which would have knocked the man unconscious and led to his death.

Cross-examined by the defence, Dr McGrath agreed that the presence of the bar in the room was consistent with it having been used as a means of supporting utensils in the small range in the room. The doctor was asked by Judge Davitt if it was his opinion that Long's head had been on the pillow in a normal sleeping position when the first blow had been struck. 'Yes,' he replied. 'The head was turned sideways.'

Sergeant Murray from Store Street station testified that when Gambon came to the station on 24 August and gave himself up he was trembling and had a wallet containing £39 in English bank notes. A further £7 in English bank notes had been given in by Mrs Gambon the previous day. Gambon next stepped into the witness box and recounted the same story he had given when he was arrested.

Concluding Gambon's defence, Mr Bell sought a verdict of manslaughter. There was no doubt that Gambon had hit Long, but there was certain provocation in the argument that took place before the fight.

Mr Justice Davitt, summing up the case, said the jury might conclude that Gambon had arranged to get his wife out of the way for the weekend, had inflicted the blows while Long was lying in bed, had taken money from a secret pocket inside Long's waistcoat, and had tried to prevent the discovery of the crime for as long as possible by locking the door. If these conclusions were the only reasonable ones that could be drawn from the facts, the judge said, then the accused man would be guilty of a particularly callous and brutal murder for robbery of a man he had called his best friend. Of course, the judge concluded, the jury must examine the facts of the case further to see if they could come to any other conclusions consistent with a less serious crime.

After retiring to deliberate, the jury came back an hour and five minutes later and found William Gambon guilty of John Long's murder. The judge said he was in complete agreement with the jury's verdict and leave to appeal the verdict was refused. When asked if he had anything to say as to why the sentence should not be passed, Gambon said, 'I have nothing to say.'

In accordance with the law, the sentence of death was passed. Gambon refused to allow his legal team to seek a reprieve and simply waited out the three weeks until his execution on 24 November 1948. Although he did not appeal his sentence, it came up for consideration by the government, which chose not to commute it to imprisonment.

A Bitter Taste

Thomas Lonergan was the son of a Kilkenny baker. As a child he showed such a thirst for knowledge that a wealthy patron offered to pay for the best education he could get and his delighted parents accepted the offer. Thomas was sent to a private school in Raheny run by Rev. Eugene McKenna and thrived in his new surroundings. After a few years he entered Trinity College and his name appears on a list of 'poor scholars' who gained admission due to their ability. When the time came to choose his path Lonergan set his heart on a career in law, but found he couldn't study it for lack of money.

Lonergan became a teacher in his old school in Raheny and also gave private lessons to the children of the well-off. In 1776, he was hired to tutor two children – John, 13, and Alice, 11 – of Thomas and Susannah O'Flaherty of Castlefield, near Thomastown, County Kilkenny. Lonergan lived with the family as a trusted guest for two years and became responsible for managing the household. He began an illicit relationship with Susannah O'Flaherty, but they were indiscrete and the affair became common knowledge in the household.

On 26 June 1778, 44-year-old Thomas O'Flaherty was in good health and spent a busy day overseeing work at his farm. He returned home at 8pm and dinner was prepared for him. The rest of the household had eaten already and the same meal was served to Thomas. It consisted of mutton hash, boiled turnips and crab meat, with custard pudding for desert. O'Flaherty ate the mutton hash and found no fault with it, but complained of the bitter taste of the turnips and the grittiness of the crab. He also ate some of the custard pudding, but complained about its taste too.

Five hours later, O'Flaherty became ill and began vomiting. A doctor was sent for, and although he didn't arrive until 8am, he brought a medicine that stopped the vomiting. Sadly, Thomas O'Flaherty's condition worsened and he died at 1am on 28 June. In the months afterwards, rumours that he had been poisoned circulated, but it was not until the spring of 1781 that suspicions became such that authorities decided to investigate.

In March 1781, Thomas Lonergan and Susannah O'Flaherty published identically worded notices in newspapers complaining that malicious rumours had been circulated that Thomas O'Flaherty had been poisoned by them and declared that they would surrender themselves at the next assizes to face trial if any charge was to be brought against them. Lonergan did surrender to the authorities, but Susannah fled the country. It is said she tricked her lover into surrendering first, promising to follow once he had made a statement.

In November, Lonergan was transferred from Kilkenny Gaol to Dublin. The trial began there on 12 November 1781, with a jury selected out of jurors from County Kilkenny. The main prosecution witnesses were Thomas O'Flaherty's children and servants from Castlefield. One remarkable feature of the trial was the appearance in the witness box of one of the jurymen, who gave evidence in favour of Lonergan, but later voted with the other jurors to find him guilty of murdering Thomas O'Flaherty by poisoning him with arsenic.

The court first heard from John Burke O'Flaherty. He told of finding his mother and Lonergan in an improper relationship. A few days before his father's death, he had witnessed him tell his mother he was going to fire Lonergan. On 26 June 1778, Lonergan had remarked to him that despite his father's good health he might be dead within the week. The 18-year-old recalled that Lonergan had brought in his father's dinner from the kitchen and had taken out the remaining turnips and crab afterwards. Lonergan had never done this before.

John said his mother had gone out with Lonergan when he brought the food away. Alice ate some of her father's custard pudding and when Susannah came back in she became angry with her daughter her for eating it, saying it was for her father. Alice became ill and began vomiting, but later recovered. After his father's death, Lonergan and his mother forced John to write to his grandmother, saying 'his father's corpse was a handsome one'. They threatened to kick him out if he did not comply. They also forced him to write letters to other people concerned about his father's death and they dictated his replies.

John told the court his father's cheeks were black at the time of his death and fluids issued from him mouth. The body was brought into the barn and covered with green sods before the burial. Sods also covered the corpse as it lay in a bedroom, and he was told it was to prevent the body swelling. Lonergan had complete control of the house after his father's death. A year later, Susannah took a house in Portarlington and she and Lonergan lived there as man and wife. She also bore him a child.

Bridget Brennan, the cook, gave testimony that Susannah and Lonergan had flaunted their relationship while her husband was alive. On the 26 June, Lonergan brought turnips into the kitchen to be reheated for Thomas O'Flaherty and waited until they were ready. He later brought the turnips and crab back to the kitchen. Lonergan had never done either before. She tasted the turnips and found them extremely bitter. She told the servants not to go near the turnips, so she could examine them the following day. The next morning they were gone and the dish they had been in was cleaned, but nobody could explain how this had happened. Brennan told the court that Thomas O'Flaherty's face had been black when he died and she believed he had been poisoned.

Brennan said the coachman, David Fitzgibbon, and a servant girl ate some of the custard pudding and became ill and began vomiting. Fitzgibbon confirmed that this had happened to him, testifying that he had eaten half a spoon of the custard, began vomiting, and remained unwell for a week afterwards. Alice O'Flaherty said she also became sick after eating some of the custard pudding and was 'roaring around the room in pain'. When she blamed the pudding, Lonergan got angry and kicked her.

Bridget Kelly, a local woman who attended dead bodies, testified that she saw O'Flaherty's corpse and it was spotted. The nails were blue and when she was fixing the shroud around his head all his hair came away. She had only ever seen such conditions in a body before when a woman had poisoned herself. She told the court that Lonergan had tried to bribe her to give evidence that the corpse looked like any corpse that had died of fevers, and that he had become angry when she refused, threatening her with jail if she said he had been poisoned.

Dr John Baker had attended Thomas O'Flaherty and initially thought he had been poisoned, but changed his mind when he went into the kitchen and found no sign of the food O'Flaherty had eaten, only clean dishes. He said if he had had any belief poison was involved, he would have reported it to the authorities at the time. It was not until several months later that he began to think O'Flaherty had taken something poisonous. When he asked Susannah for permission to exhume the body, she had refused. Asked by a member of the jury if O'Flaherty's hair falling off, his nails turning black and the 'livid spots so soon after death' – added to the symptoms before his death – were signs of poisoning, Dr Baker said they were.

For the defence, three witnesses sought to undermine John Burke O'Flaherty's testimony. They claimed he had told them he did not believe his father had been poisoned and had never witnessed any intimacy between Lonergan and his mother. These witnesses were all relations of Susannah O'Flaherty. The undertaker, Edward Keary testified that the corpse appeared like any other, but then admitted he had not examined it. He noted he had taken the body out of a pit in a barn, which he had never heard of before.

After an hour's deliberation, the jury found Thomas Lonergan guilty of murder and sentenced him to be hung, drawn and quartered at St Stephen's Green on 24 November 1781. Lonergan admitted that he had bought the arsenic at Susannah's direction to kill rats, but he did not confess his guilt.

Rev. McKenna did not forget his former pupil and assistant. He visited him in prison, was a character witness at the trial, and after Lonergan had been sentenced to death, saw to his spiritual needs. In his book, *Twenty Years' Recollections of an Irish Police Magistrate* (1880), Frank Thorpe Porter gives an account of the execution and extraordinary aftermath as told to him by his father, who was a close friend of Rev. McKenna and knew Lonergan. Porter's father was a sergeant of the Dublin Volunteers and attended the execution in charge of a company of soldiers.

Lonergan was conveyed to the gallows at St Stephen's Green in a cart, escorted by a troop of cavalry. The condemned man remained on the cart when it stopped under the gallows. When the noose was properly adjusted round his neck, the cart was driven away, leaving Lonergan dangling on the gallows. Lonergan did not get much of a drop, but he almost immediately ceased to struggle and appeared to be dead. The December weather was extremely bad, and when the body had been hanging for twenty minutes the sheriff allowed it to be cut down. The quartering part of the sentence was complied with when the hangman made two incisions with a sharp knife across the back of the neck.

The body was then handed over to Rev. McKenna, who placed it in a coffin that had been waiting in a hearse. The remains were brought out to his house in Raheny. A funeral service was held and the coffin was buried in Raheny graveyard in the presence of a small group of mourners. A guard was kept at the grave for several nights in case any grave robbers attempted to exhume the body and sell it to be anatomised by surgeons.

Two days later, Sergeant Porter received a note from Rev. McKenna asking him to come to Raheny. He was sworn to secrecy and asked to help his friend with a problem. Porter agreed and was led up to an attic room where he was surprised to see Lonergan alive – but very weak after his experience at the gallows. A few days later, Porter brought Lonergan to his own house in Skinner's Row and hid him for several days until he was well enough to travel. The two men succeeded in getting Lonergan to Bristol and then to America, where he settled down under the name James Fennell and lived as a school teacher.

Lonergan attributed his survival to the rope being unusually short and his being swung from the cart without receiving any drop. He said that on being hanged he immediately lost all consciousness. Porter recorded that 'his revival was attended with violent and distressing convulsions'.

The Madness of Inspector Montgomery

Imagine a situation where a person commits murder and is then put in charge of the investigation to find the killer. It sounds like fiction, but it actually happened in Newtownstewart in County Tyrone in 1871, when bank cashier William Glass was murdered by District Inspector Thomas Montgomery!

At 4pm on 29 June 1871, Fanny McBride was passing through the hall of the Northern Banking Company premises when she noticed blood flowing out from under the closed door of an outer office. McBride worked as a maid for the bank manager and had come downstairs to check the time on the bank's clock. The alarm was raised immediately and the dead body of 25-year-old William Glass was found lying in a pool of blood. He had been savagely beaten. His head had numerous deep cuts and a sharp-pointed copper file had been driven from ear-to-ear through his head.

The bank safe was lying open and it was later established that £1,600 in cash and gold had been taken. The police were called and Inspector Montgomery arrived at the scene and took charge. To the surprise of all present, he suggested that Glass had committed suicide. Others pointed out that it was unlikely Glass had inflicted such injuries on himself. Montgomery then ordered a search for the murderer.

William Glass

Inspector Thomas Montgomery

He horrified his subordinates by having the body removed from the crime scene and not following protocol by alerting all local police stations of the murder. Instead, he telegraphed neighbouring District Inspector William Purcell in Omagh, asking him to 'Please inform the coroner that a death under suspicious circumstances has occurred, and I request his attendance as soon as possible here.' He later sent a message by train to headquarters reporting that 'William Glass, bank cashier, murdered, and large sum of money stolen; please examine trains and lodging-houses.'

Near midnight he told his men he was going home for a few hours' sleep, but instead went to a wooded area outside Newtownstewart known as Grangewood. At 2am, he met Inspector Purcell coming from Omagh to help and explained that he was keeping an eye on the property of the Great Northern Railway in case strikers caused any damage. Purcell

Inspector Montgomery murders William Glass.

and Montgomery walked into town together and discussed the murder. He asked Purcell, 'Could the last person coming out of the bank be convicted if he had no blood on his clothes?' and Purcell answered that 'He thought not.'

The significance of the question would become apparent when it was discovered that Montgomery was the last person seen coming out of the bank. Three days later, he was arrested for the murder of his friend William Glass. Several people had seen Inspector Montgomery near the bank around the time of the murder, and police discovered that he had motive, as his finances were extremely unhealthy.

There was no sign of the murder weapon or the stolen money until nearly six months later, when a boy hunting rabbits with his dog in Grangewood came across bank notes washed out of their hiding place by rain. A search uncovered more than £1,500 in cash and £30 in gold hidden under a large stone. Nearby, a bill hook heavily weighted with lead was discovered. It was later established this weapon was also used in the murder.

Thomas Montgomery stood trial in Omagh in July 1872 and cut a handsome figure in the dock. The prosecution's case was that Montgomery had waited until a day he knew the bank manager, Mr J. G. Strahan, was at a sub-office in Drumquin for the weekly fair, and he had then killed Glass and stolen the money. Montgomery was a close friend to the younger man and was helping him apply for a career in the police. He was a regular visitor to the bank and Glass trusted him. Strahan's family was away on holidays, leaving only his aunt, a Miss Thompson, the maid, Fanny McBride, and the gardener, Robert Cooke, at the bank.

Around 2.30pm, Miss Thompson was in the manager's home above the bank when there was a knock at the door and Inspector Montgomery entered. He wondered if Strahan was about and would like to go fishing. When she said he would not be back until 6pm, Montgomery left. A little before this time, one of the last customers in the bank heard Glass speaking to someone in an inner office. The bank shut at 3pm, but it seems likely Montgomery bolted shut its doors earlier.

Although several people saw Montgomery leave the bank around 3.30pm, only three gave evidence in court. The first was Mary Ann Cameron, and her evidence was extremely dubious. The second was Harriet McDowell, who ran a shop directly across from the bank with her husband James. She gave clear testimony that Inspector Montgomery left the bank at 3.20pm and shut the door behind him. He was wearing a round hat and dark clothes, and had a waterproof coat on his arm and a stick in one hand.

The third person who saw Montgomery leave the bank about this time was James McDowell, who testified that he saw Montgomery come out of the bank at the time his wife said and had previously sold Montgomery a few pounds of lead. The policeman had told McDowell he wanted to make bullets, but no lead or bullet mould was found at Montgomery's residence. The prosecution asserted that he had bought the lead to weight the bill hook.

A policeman testified that Montgomery had previously told him how strange it was that no one had tried to rob a bank, adding that it easily could be done by knocking the cashier on the head and escaping. The bank manager, Strahan, told the court Montgomery had once asked what would stop anyone coming in, killing the man in charge, and robbing the bank. Strahan had flourished his pistol and said he would use it on any thief. But Strahan always took the pistol with him to Drumquin.

The prosecution was unable to show that Montgomery had a motive for killing Glass and robbing the bank, as the judge refused to allow them put forward evidence to show that Montgomery was in desperate financial straits. It is hard to understand this decision. The defence later urged the jury to acquit Montgomery, as the prosecution had shown no motive for the crime. Nine jurors voted to convict Montgomery and three were for acquittal. A retrial was ordered.

At the second trial, evidence of Montgomery's perilous finances was admitted, despite the defence's objections. Montgomery was heavily in debt to his father-in-law and had embezzled several hundred pounds from his constables, on the pretext of investing it for them. Montgomery was in danger of being dismissed from the police and prosecuted for fraud if he could not pay the money back.

It looked like Montgomery would be convicted of the murder, but the prosecution cleverly sowed the seeds of doubt in some jurors' minds by asking how, if Montgomery was the murderer, he could have taken the money out of the bank and concealed the weapon in broad daylight, as both were bulky items. Some of the jurors agreed that this was an issue, and asked to see Montgomery's clothing to help them understand how he might have concealed bundles of money and the weapon. Ultimately, two jurors voted for acquittal.

Four months later, on 21 July 1873, the third trial began and the prosecution cleverly rebutted the defence's suggestion that it was impossible for Montgomery to have left the bank with the money and weapon and not be seen. The prosecution called in a police officer of the same build of Montgomery, wearing the very clothes the inspector had on 29 June 1871 and stood him on a table, holding an overcoat on his arm.

The court gasped when it heard the man had the same amount of money stolen from the bank tucked into his clothes and the murder weapon in his pocket. The policeman could move freely and no one would have guessed what was packed around his person. As requested the policeman slowly took out the notes in bundles and placed them on a table. Then pulled out the bill hook and laid it down too, destroying Montgomery's hopes of an acquittal. It took the jury fifteen minutes to find him guilty of William Glass's murder.

When asked if he had anything to say before the sentence was passed, the guilty man made an extraordinary speech.

He confessed to the murder but said he had been insane at the time. He claimed his father-in-law had drugged and poisoned him a year before the murder and he had foolishly gambled large sums of money. 'I became vicious, and this mono-mania for attacking banks took possession of me,' he claimed. This attempt to escape execution fooled no one, and Montgomery was sentenced to death.

While he awaited execution, he was interviewed in his cell by the press. He cleared up several points about the murder. By the time he saw Miss Thompson, the murder had been committed and the money and weapon were concealed about him. His bloody hands had been in his pockets while speaking to her, but he had sponged the blood of his coat and trousers. 'Poor Glass,' he declared, 'didn't speak at all after he was struck. He had an easy time of it.' Montgomery repeated his claim that he had been drugged into insanity by his father-in-law. Asked if he had any hope of a reprieve on the grounds of insanity, he replied, 'No, I don't think so.'

Thomas Montgomery was hanged at Omagh Gaol on 26 August 1873. His last words were to the executioner. He asked, 'Is hanging painful?'

The Girl who Fell from the Sky

When the body of a young woman – naked except for a pair of briefs – washed ashore at Doolin Strand in County Clare and was discovered by local fishermen on 24 May 1967, gardaí were immediately alerted. Detective Superintendent John Butler arrived and took charge of the scene. The state pathologist, Dr Maurice Hickey, carefully examined the body and reported his findings.

The woman had been beaten, her clothes had been ripped off during a struggle, and then she had died after falling from a great height onto rocks, Dr Hickey reported. It was some small mercy that she would have died instantly on impact.

All signs indicated that the woman had been murdered. Her clothes were never recovered, and no one had seen her in the locality. Her identity was a mystery, but it was likely she was a tourist. The girl was in her late twenties, very pretty and tanned, had excellent teeth and her hands were soft and manicured. Her underwear was made in America, which indicated that she was not Irish. Detective Butler suggested that the unknown woman had most likely been pushed off the 700-foot-high Cliffs of Moher.

The body would then have drifted across the bay to Doolin. The woman's badly damaged face was reconstructed by a mortician and her photograph was placed in the national newspapers, but no one came forward to identify her. Gardaí received two leads that looked promising, but proved to be dead ends.

The first suggested that the mystery woman had been with two men in a helicopter that had landed on the nearby Aran Islands the day before the body had been discovered. But gardaí located that woman and those men, and this put an end to the far-fetched theory that the mystery woman had been thrown out of a helicopter. The second was from a receptionist at a hotel in Lisdonvarna who claimed the photograph looked like an American tourist who had checked out on 23 May, but this woman was quickly located too.

The first solid lead came when gardaí searching the Cliffs of Moher made two finds near O'Brien's Tower. They found a gold bracelet stained with blood and a woman's left shoe. Both were of American origin and the shoe fitted the victim. A local woman had been awake in the early hours of 23 May and had noticed the lights of a car parked in the field a short distance from the cliffside, between 3am and 4am. The lights had stayed on for ten minutes and then disappeared. The woman had thought it strange and had come forward when the body had been discovered.

On 1 June 1967, the unknown American girl was buried in a simple coffin at Drumcliffe Cemetery in Ennis. The only mourners were a handful of gardaí. The day before the lonely funeral, a seemingly unrelated event occurred in New York that would lead to the solving of the baffling mystery of the unknown woman. Fifty-two-year-old Virginia Domenech failed to show up for work at a children's home in the Bronx, where she was as a social worker. This was unusual, but her supervisor and friend thought Virginia might have gone to

Maria Domenech

the airport to pick up her 28-year-old daughter, Maria, who had been in Europe on holidays for two weeks and was due to return home on 31 May.

For two days the supervisor was unable to reach Virginia or her daughter, and so she went around to their apartment. When no one answered, Maria became worried, sought out the building superintendent and voiced her concerns. He had not seen Virginia in several days and reported her disappearance on 4 June. He also phoned Virginia's brother Juan Goya in Puerto Rico. Goya got the next flight to New York and went straight to the police.

They went with him to the apartment and went in. It looked like no one had been there for several days. There was food in the fridge and rubbish to be taken out, but no sign of any struggle. A newspaper dated 30 May lay in the apartment. It looked as if Virginia had stepped out and never returned. Juan Goya became extremely worried about his sister and her daughter. In a pile of mail was a postcard from Maria from Paris, dated 22 May, saying she would write a letter to her mother.

There was no sign of this letter in the apartment. The Domenechs had lived there for five years and were very pleasant by all accounts. Despite being wealthy, they both worked as social workers by choice. Neighbours had last seen Virginia on 30 May. Police discovered that Maria had a boyfriend called Roberto Martin and were alarmed to discover that he had been worried about her when she had failed to arrive at Kennedy Airport on 31 May. He had tried to reach Maria's brother, but he had gone to Puerto Rico on holiday.

He also told police that she had once been involved with an older man, but he did not know his name. Police returned to the apartment and found a locked drawer that had not been examined. Opening it, they saw it was in disarray as if it had been ransacked.

The detective in charge of the case, Lieutenant Francis Sullivan, theorised that Maria had come to harm abroad and the killer had raced back and killed Virginia and taken the letter to insure his identity remained unknown. The most likely motive was money – Maria had taken more than $6,000 with her in cash and traveller's cheques.

In Paris, Chief Inspector Georges Durr traced Maria's movements in the city. A hotel receptionist recalled that she had stayed there on 21 May but had checked out the next day. An American man in his forties had come to the desk that night looking for Maria and they had greeted each other like close friends. Durr failed to find the flight Maria had departed France on and guessed that she and her friend had travelled under false names.

In New York, Lieutenant Sullivan spoke to Maria's brother by phone from Puerto Rico and learned important information. He had received a card from his sister posted at Orly Airport near Paris on 22 May, in which she mentioned that she had decided to visit London and Dublin. Sullivan went back and interviewed Virginia's friend at the children's home in the hopes of identifying any male friends of hers who had been previously overlooked.

Eventually, the woman remembered briefly meeting a Patrick Darcy. He was traced and, when questioned, admitted knowing Virginia, but said he had not seen her for several months. Darcy was a travel agent and regularly went to Europe, but said he had not left New York recently. Next, Sullivan contacted his counterparts in Scotland Yard in London and Garda Headquarters in Dublin, asking them to look for any trace of Maria Domenech and the unknown man travelling with her.

As Maria had been fingerprinted for her job, Sullivan was able to provide a set of prints alongside a photograph. Chief Superintendent Patrick McLaughlin of the Garda Technical Bureau in Dublin immediately noticed that the description and photograph of Maria Domenech closely matched those of the unknown girl in Clare and a fingerprint match confirmed his suspicion. Superintendent Butler had been making little progress on the case for six weeks when this welcome news reached him.

Butler wondered how Maria had travelled from Paris to London to Dublin and then made the 150-mile journey to the Cliffs of Moher, and guessed that she must have flown directly to Shannon Airport, only 30 miles away. This would help narrow the search considerably. For the moment, news of the identification of the body was not released, for fear of tipping off the killer. Instead, gardaí quietly conducted a huge search of flight and hotel records for some trace of Maria and her killer.

On 15 August 1967, Sergeant Michael Purcell of the immigration department at Shannon Airport spotted a discrepancy while searching hotel records gathered by the gardaí. He noticed that an 'A. Young' had booked into Shannon International Hotel at 8am on 23 May and had checked out at midday. Most airline passengers passing through Shannon took a room to rest and freshen up while waiting for a flight, but 'A. Young' did not appear on any passenger lists for flights arriving or departing that day. This meant that the man had arrived by car. Purcell checked the hotel garage and found that his hunch was correct.

The hotel routinely took down car registrations, and Detective Butler was able to track this vehicle to a Dublin car-hire company. He established that Young had rented the car at 11pm on 22 May and returned it the following day after clocking up 320 miles. Further investigations established that an 'A. Young' and a 'Miss M. Young' had flown from Paris to London, then on to Dublin, arriving on the evening of 22 May. 'A. Young' had departed Dublin for Paris on 23 May, but it appeared 'Miss M. Young' had never left Ireland.

When Lieutenant Sullivan learned of the results of the Garda investigations, he was convinced the killer was known to the Domenechs and concentrated his investigation on their male friends. Sullivan suspected that Young was a false name and was proved correct when people at the New York address Young had given said no one by that name was known there.

All he had was a sample of the handwriting that 'A. Young' had given at the Shannon hotel and the Dublin car-hire firm. All of Maria's male friends were cleared, including Roberto Martin, when it was established that none of them could have been in Ireland on 22–23 May.

The policeman recalled that 47-year-old Patrick Darcy had mentioned meeting her through Maria when she had worked for an airline at the New York World's Fair. Sullivan wondered how well he had known Maria. Roberto Martin had mentioned she had once been involved with an older man and Sullivan wondered if Darcy was that man.

He spoke to a close friend of Maria's and asked if she had ever met Patrick Darcy. This friend confirmed that Maria had been involved with him when she first arrived in New York, but had found out he was married and ended the relationship. Sullivan wondered if Darcy had turned his attentions to her attractive mother. An investigation of Darcy yielded valuable information. He was the son of Irish immigrants, was familiar with Ireland, and had travelled extensively in Europe in connection with his travel business.

He also had other possibly murkier interests, as he sometimes travelled under the names of 'A. Young' and 'John J. Quinn' and had travel documents in both these names. He travelled to Miami frequently and may have been involved in illegal activities. His travel business was not going well and, more significantly, he had been absent from New York in late May despite what he had told Sullivan.

Darcy had returned a few days before the disappearance of Virginia Domenech. Also, his description matched that of the 'A. Young' who had briefly stayed at the Shannon Hotel. Police in New York also learned that Maria had cashed in $2,000 worth of traveller's cheques at London Airport. New York police could only question Darcy about Virginia Domenech's disappearance until an extradition request came from Ireland relating to Maria's murder.

Darcy was confident under repeated questioning by Sullivan. Handwriting experts matched the 'A. Young' signatures from the Irish hotel and car-hire firm to his, but Darcy denied that the handwriting was his and insisted he was not 'A. Young'. He claimed he had not travelled with Maria to Ireland, but had to admit he had been abroad for at least a week in late May.

When Sullivan accused him of killing Maria and Virginia, Darcy claimed to know nothing about Maria's death or her mother's disappearance. He refused to answer any more questions and the police had to let him go. Although Darcy was under constant surveillance, he gave police the slip on 11 October and disappeared.

When Darcy could not be found, Sullivan guessed he had gone to Miami and requested that police there locate him. Detective Sergeant Charles Shepherd was examining hotel registrations at the McAllister Hotel when he spotted Darcy's alias 'John J. Quinn'. Shepherd and the hotel manager went to the man's room and knocked, but there was no response. When they opened the door, they found Patrick Darcy lying on the bed dead. He had committed suicide by taking barbiturates and drinking a bottle of whiskey. He had left two suicide notes, but these failed to shed any new light on the death of Maria or the disappearance of her mother.

Apparently Darcy had chosen to end his life rather than face the bleak future that lay ahead. He would have been arrested and extradited to Ireland to face trial for Maria's murder. With Darcy's death, police considered the murder of Maria Domenech closed, but they never discovered what happened to Virginia Domenech. Maria's body was disinterred from its grave in Ennis and reburied in her native Puerto Rico.

Burial at Dawn

Hangman James Berry executed more than 130 murderers, and he regarded Dr Philip Cross as the bravest of them. 'Of all the men I hanged, Dr Cross was the only one who walked firmly to the scaffold,' Berry later wrote, adding that Cross had told the prison staff he did not fear death, for he had faced it more than once on the battlefield. He calmly walked to the gallows and died without any final words. This brave man was also a callous killer, who had cruelly poisoned his wife so he could marry his lover.

Philip Cross was from an affluent background. His family resided near Coachford, County Cork, at Shandy Hall, a fine Georgian mansion set in an estate of several hundred acres. After studying medicine at the Royal College of Surgeons in Dublin, Cross joined the British Army in 1848 and embarked on a military career, fighting around the world, including in the Crimean War and the Indian Mutiny. He eventually rose to the rank of surgeon-major.

In 1869, when he was 46-years-old, Cross met and fell in love with 29-year-old English heiress Mary Laura Marriott. Despite her parents' disproval, the couple married at St James's Church in Piccadilly, London, in August the same year. A few days later the couple left for Canada so Cross could re-join his regiment. Mary's father died the following year, leaving her

Dr Cross with Effie Skinner.

the considerable sum of £5,000. She and Cross returned to London in 1875, and a year later Cross retired from the army when his father died and left him Shandy Hall.

They moved to Coachford and settled down in the Cork countryside to raise their six children. Dr Cross was not a popular figure in the locality due to his abrasive manner and rough ways. When a neighbouring farmer objected to Cross hunting across his land Cross gave the man such a blow that his ear was torn off. Cross's victim was awarded £200 in damages, which, though a large sum of money, was poor recompense for such an injury. Cross was afterwards banned from the local hunt.

Mary Cross suffered from poor health and was an epileptic. In November 1886, she hired 20-year-old Effie Skinner, a clergyman's daughter from Scotland, as a governess to look after the children. Cross, who was then 63 years old, became infatuated with the young girl, brazenly seizing her in his arms and kissing her one day when they were alone. Effie said nothing to her mistress, and Dr Cross continued his advances and a relationship seems to have developed.

By the following January, Mary Cross became aware of the relationship and fired Effie. She paid the younger woman's train fare to Dublin and provided her with a reference for a new job in Carlow. Instead of taking up a new position, Effie stayed in a Dublin hotel paid for by Philip Cross. He began a secret correspondence with her, sending a servant to the post office with his letters, and collecting the replies himself.

Cross sometimes made trips to Dublin to see Effie, telling his wife it was for business. On at least two occasions, the lovers stayed in Dublin hotels together, signing in as husband and wife. Effie became pregnant and Dr Cross was determined to marry the young woman, but first he had to get his wife out of the way. Instead of seeking a scandalous divorce, the doctor decided to kill the mother of his six children.

Although her health had never been great, by the middle of
May 1887 Mary Cross's condition had seriously deteriorated
and she was bedridden. She suffered from debilitating
spasms, stomach cramps, irritated eyes and diarrhoea until
her death. Dr Cross oversaw her treatment and said she was
suffering from a 'bilious fever', possibly typhoid. For a long
time, he did not call in any other doctor.

Two weeks after Mary had become seriously ill,
however, Cross relented and called in a younger cousin,
Dr Thomas Godfrey, to examine her. Godfrey deferred to
Cross's experience and concurred with his opinion. Despite
Cross's efforts to keep visitors away, the local doctor called
unannounced and would not leave. After briefly examining
Mary, he agreed that she was suffering from a bilious fever.
Dr Cross dutifully cared for his wife night and day, but her
condition continued to worsen.

When family friends called he told them she was no
better. The local clergyman, Rev. Hayes, also visited, but
he was told Mary was asleep and could not be disturbed.
On the night of 1 June, a servant heard Mary Cross get sick
in her bedroom. This was followed by several screams, then
silence. Dr Cross roused the servants on the morning of 2
June, brusquely telling them, 'Get up girls – the Missus is
gone since past one last night.' They were surprised by his
manner and would later say he did not act like a man who
had lost his wife.

Poor Mary Cross was hardly cold when her husband
signed the death certificate himself, declaring that she had
died from typhoid fever. He buried his wife with 'indecent
haste' at 6am on 4 June, with only himself and two others
present. In his diary Cross wrote, 'Mary Laura Cross

departed this life, 2nd. May she go to heaven is my prayer. Buried on 4th.' Two days later he recorded the cost of her funeral: five guineas. He had given her the cheapest funeral possible.

News of the bizarre funeral shocked many, even though Dr Cross explained that it had been done to prevent the spread of the disease. The following day, Cross left for England to give the dreadful news to his children at their schools. He also had an ulterior motive. Some weeks before, Cross had sent Effie to England. Fifteen days after the funeral, he married her at St James's Church in Piccadilly, the same place he had married Mary.

News of the wedding preceded Dr Cross and his new bride when they returned to Shandy Hall two weeks later. It is not surprising that rumours of foul play quickly reached the police. When Inspector Henry Tyacke investigated, he was shocked to find that Dr Cross had signed the death certificate himself. After interviewing the Crosses' servants, friends, and neighbours, Inspector Tyacke obtained an order to exhume the body, referring to Mary Cross's death, the hasty funeral, and her husband's speedy remarriage. It did not help Cross's case that there had been no cases of typhoid in the Coachford area for decades.

An autopsy showed no signs of typhoid fever, but high levels of arsenic and strychnine. It appeared that the poor woman had been slowly poisoned with the former and finished off with the latter. She had suffered a terrible death. Philip Cross was arrested on 28 July 1887 and jailed. His trial began on 14 December. Demand for seats at the trial was such that admission to the court had to be ticketed. Several thousand people applied.

The trial lasted four days before Dr Cross was found guilty of his wife's murder and sentenced to death. Effie, who had refused to have anything to do with him since the murder had been discovered, gave birth to their son John Cross on 23 December. Dr Cross was hanged at Cork Gaol on 10 January 1888. Even though he had killed their mother, Cross's older children supported his plea for a reprieve. By the time he was executed, his hair had turned white.

The Informer

When the body of a young Italian organ grinder, Domenico Garlibardo, was found on the banks of the River Dodder, near Rathfarnham, on 28 February 1841 one newspaper dubbed it 'one of the most horrible and cold-blooded murders perpetrated in this country for the last century'. The 22-year-old had been attacked and viciously murdered. His throat had been cut and all his money stolen.

At first, suspicion fell on three Italians Garlibardo lived with, but then a couple from Terenure called Richard and Mary Cooney were accused of the murder. Cooney stood trial but was acquitted. A reward of £25 had been advertised for the conviction of Garlibardo's murderer, and this had tempted 20-year-old John Delahunt to come forward and testify that he had seen Cooney murder the Italian youth. Fortunately for Cooney, the jury did not believe Delahunt. One writer would later suggest that if Delahunt knew anything about the crime it was because he was the killer.

Four months after the trial, a retired soldier called Captain Craddock was dragged out of his bed and beaten up by a gang that had broken into his house on Meath Street. They were coal porters from the city quays who had been hired by a candidate running for election in Dublin to intimidate people into voting for him. When Craddock refused to comply, they assaulted him.

A reward was offered for the discovery and conviction of the men and Delahunt lost no time coming forward as a witness again. He pointed out six random coal porters on the quays of Dublin and the unfortunate men were arrested and sent for trial. Delahunt took to the stand and swore he had been present when the men had attacked Craddock, but had not taken part in the assault. Under cross-examination his story was torn apart.

It did not help that Captain Craddock was adamant that one of the men, who had a harelip, had not been present. Another accused man had actually been in jail on a charge of being drunk and disorderly at the time Delahunt claimed he had attacked Craddock. All six men were acquitted. Counsel on both sides agreed that Delahunt had not been present at the assault, but had come forward to claim the reward by convicting innocent persons.

John Delahunt's third attempt to claim a reward was far more sinister. Nine-year-old Thomas Maguire lived with his mother in Plunkett Street. On the afternoon of 20 December 1841, he received permission from his mother to go play with some other children in Blackhall Row. At 4pm, the children were busy playing when a man arrived and called to Thomas by his name. They spoke for a moment and Thomas went away with the man. The children would later identify this person as John Delahunt.

Where they went for the next two hours is uncertain, but at 6pm Delahunt and the boy arrived at his brother's house in Britain Street. Delahunt told his sister-in-law that he had found the boy lost near Dublin Castle and had been asked by Colonel Brown, a police commissioner they knew, to bring the boy home to his parents on Buckingham Street.

Delahunt's kind-hearted sister-in-law asked Thomas if he was hungry, made him sit down at the fire and gave him something to eat.

Then, saying he was bringing the boy home, Delahunt took Maguire and left his brother's. But he didn't bring him home. Delahunt took the boy to Drake's public house on Capel Street for a short while. The next place they were seen was at Upper Baggot Street, which was about 2 miles from Capel Street, not far from Delahunt's father's home at Eastmoreland Place. Delahunt was met by his sister and two or three young children, and one asked where he was going. Delahunt replied that he had found the boy lost at Dublin Castle and was bringing him to his parents' home. After he left his sister, Delahunt headed in the direction of Ballsbridge. It was then about a quarter to seven. Twenty minutes later he arrived at his father's house, without the child.

A little while later, Thomas Maguire was found murdered at the rear of stables on Pembroke Lane, behind Pembroke Road, a short distance from the spot where Delahunt had met his sister. The boy's body was still warm, with blood still pouring from a dreadful wound on his neck.

Before Delahunt left his father's house, he promised to return in two or three days to be present at some entertainment to be given by some children he was friendly with. He then went to Dublin Castle and gave information about witnessing the murder of the child in the place where his body was found. He led a policeman to the spot.

When they arrived, local police from Baggot Street station were already making enquiries. At the station, Delahunt calmly gave a detailed description of the murder he had witnessed. His testimony would have caused the mother of the murdered boy to be arrested for killing her own son. Unluckily for Delahunt, Thomas Maguire's mother had an alibi. At 5pm the same evening she had gone to the lying-in hospital where she gave birth to a child.

Having led the police officer to the murder scene, Delahunt left him and went back to his brother's house on Britain Street. When asked where he had left the child he replied he had left the boy at Buckingham Street, where the boy said he could find his way home from. A few days after the murder some boys playing in a field near to where the murder took place, found a knife, which was later proved to belong to Delahunt's brother. Delahunt's sister-in-law testified that the accused man had sharpened it a few days before the murder and it had subsequently gone missing. Once police realised that Delahunt's statement was false, they arrested him for the murder of poor Thomas Maguire. Delahunt stood trial for the boy's murder on 17 January 1842. In the dock he looked pale and haggard, and he was clearly extremely anxious. He leaned forward on his elbows throughout the trial, with a handkerchief in his hand covering his lower face, and remained this way throughout the proceedings.

Delahunt pleaded not guilty, but once the prosecution had detailed their case, backed up with witnesses – mostly from his own family – it only took the jury only twenty minutes to find him guilty of the horrible crime. Delahunt displayed no emotion when he heard the verdict, but when the judge asked if he had anything to say about why he should not be executed for the crime, Delahunt, deathly pale, replied in a faint voice, 'I am not guilty.'

When the judge sentenced him to hang at the front of Kilmainham Gaol on 5 February 1842, Delahunt fainted and did not recover for several minutes. A few days before the execution he made a confession to a priest of his crimes and it was taken down in front of witnesses. He said he had nothing to do with the murder of Domenico Garlibardo but that he had falsely accused Cooney, and he said his evidence against the coal porters was similarly false. He had perjured himself in the hopes of earning a reward.

The most chilling part of his statement related to the murder of Maguire, who Delahunt admitted he had killed to earn a reward for convicting the child's mother of the murder. 'I kept him nearly half an hour in the lane,' Delahunt said. 'He twice asked me was I coming home soon, as his mother would be beating him. I said I was waiting for a jaunting car. He spent part of the time sitting in the corner at the stable door on a heap of dung or litter heaped up outside.'

Delahunt calmly recalled the actual murder in a matter-of-fact manner. 'I was then turning in my mind how I could best cut his throat. He stood up by my side. I felt his throat, and asked him had he lumps in his throat. He made no reply. After some minutes I again felt his throat with my left hand, having the knife in my right hand ready. My right hand was then down in my coat pocket, when I asked him a second time had he lumps in his throat, and began again to feel him. He raised up his head to let me feel more easily. His back was then to me, and at that moment, while he was in that position, with his head drawn back, I cut his throat, and threw him from me,' Delahunt's statement said. 'He fell on his face. He uttered no cry, nor did he make any noise whatever. On getting three yards from him I looked back, and saw him on his feet again going in the direction of the cottage in the field.'

As to why he choose to kill a child, Delahunt explained that he was 'afraid to attack a large person, and the boy being small and weak suited my purpose'.

The day before his execution Delahunt said his goodbyes to his parents and two brothers and two sisters. This last meeting was described by one newspaper as 'truly heart-rending'. A priest was on hand to console the family and he remained with Delahunt after they left. Resigned to his fate Delahunt had a light meal of tea and bread. After saying his payers at 11pm the condemned man slept peacefully for several hours.

The next morning he had a hearty breakfast and said more prayers. His arms were pinioned and he was brought out to the execution platform at 12pm. A crowd of over 20,000 people had gathered to witness the execution and they watched in silence. On seeing the executioner, Delahunt fainted. He was revived, the noose and a cap were quickly put on and he was placed on the drop. At this point Delahunt's courage failed him and he fainted again, collapsing onto the trap door. The executioner tried to get him to stand up, but eventually gave up and pulled the trapdoor lever.

One Sock

Edward Lindsay was a well-known eccentric from Armagh town. The 70-year-old lived alone in the imposing Killuney Lodge on Portadown Road. Lindsay was variously described as a retired miller or a travelling salesman. In his youth he had been a well-dressed and connected member of society, but he had become something of a recluse and hoarder in his later years and had allowed his lovely house to fall into disrepair. Despite his eccentricities, Lindsay was a popular figure in the town and the alarm was raised on 6 December 1908, when a young girl saw that the milk she had delivered the two previous days had not been taken inside.

The police were called and, after getting no response when they knocked and shouted, broke into the house and made a search for the missing man. In a darkened bedroom they discovered what they initially thought was a pile of old clothes lying in the middle of the floor. After letting light in, they saw a pair of feet sticking out of the pile. Buried beneath the clothes was the body of Edward Lindsay, lying on its back. A loaded pistol lay beside it.

Officers immediately saw that the poor man had been stabbed in the head several times. There were cuts on his hands, indicating that he had tried to defend himself. It was plain to see he had died in agony. The room had been

Edward Lindsay

ransacked and drawers had been pulled out and their contents scattered on the floor. The scene looked like a burglary gone wrong. It was not immediately clear what had been taken, but neighbours reported that Lindsay always wore a gold watch, and there was no sign of it.

Over the years, Lindsay had become progressively odder and took less care of himself. He was blind in one eye from a cataract. His usual habit was to stay in bed until 3pm and then walk to a neighbour's well a short distance away and draw water. The last time he had been seen alive was on 4 December at about 3pm. The police investigation concluded that Lindsay had been murdered about half an hour after that. Around 3.30pm, a man named Cassells passing by the house saw a man looking out of one of the windows. A few minutes later, schoolgirls passing by on the way home heard the cries of murder. They heard Lindsay shout, 'How did you get in?' and sounds of a fight and two gunshots. Then Lindsay cried out, 'Will nobody help me?' They ran home and told their parents, who thought it was just Lindsay acting crazy.

The inquest concluded that Lindsay had been stabbed five times in the forehead. His skull was cracked and he had died from blood loss when an artery had been cut. The police concluded that Lindsay had returned home after drawing water and found the intruder in his house and fired his revolver at him, but missed due to his poor eyesight. He had been attacked and killed before he could fire again. The burglar had then quickly ransacked the room before fleeing.

Police learned that staff at the Northern Hotel in Armagh had taken note of a man who had tried to sell a barman a gold watch on 5 December. He had also offered the watch to a patron in the bar and this man, Thomas Horan, told police it was engraved 'J.C. Quail'. Police established that this watch had been Lindsay's. Horan said he had been offered it by a man called Oliver Curran and gave police a description of him.

Curran was a blacksmith from Ardee, County Louth, who lived a vagrant existence. Shortly before the murder he had borrowed a small sum of money from a friend, but afterwards he suddenly had in his possession several pounds. He stayed in Armagh until 6 December then left for Newry.

Oliver Curran

There he asked a railway official what time a boat next went to England. Hearing it would not leave for another two days Curran waited a day and booked a ticket for Dundalk, which also had a port.

A policeman on duty at Newry station spotted the black-bearded man at the ticket office and realised that he matched the wanted man's description. He promptly arrested Curran and brought him to the Newry police station. In one of his pockets, Curran had Edward Lindsay's gold watch. He was wearing a vest, trousers and boots belonging to Lindsay, and a sock that was identified as the companion of one found in Lindsay's house. A bloodstained dagger with a recently broken point was in another pocket. Curran had tried to clean it but minute pieces of flesh were found on its blade. The trousers Curran wore had blood on them too, and it matched Edward Lindsay's.

Curran refused to answer questions from the police about the killing of the elderly man, and he was charged with murder on 9 March 1909 in Armagh. The defence at first tried to plead that Curran was insane, but a jury found he was not. So another jury was sworn in and the case was tried. The evidence was stacked against the 35-year-old Curran. In particular, he had been seen by William McGahey heading towards Lindsay's house before 3pm. He also had been seen looking out from a window by Cassells at 3.30pm, and another man, William Mansbridge, had seen him leaving Killuney Lodge at 5pm.

Oliver Curran was found guilty but insane, and sent to Dundrum Criminal Lunatic Asylum in Dublin, where more than a third of the 300 or so inmates were killers. One of the oldest detainees was 84-year-old John Fitzsimons, who had killed his son. On 23 July 1911 Fitzsimons was attacked with a lead-weighted brush used to clean the floors and he died the following day.

During the investigation into the murder, Curran was questioned and bloody white hairs were found sticking to his shoes. He admitted to the killing, saying he had kicked the elderly man in the head and also used the brush. Curran appeared in court for the murder on 1 August 1911 and the prosecution stated that he was insane and unfit to plead. He was returned to the asylum.

Trial by Battle

Trial by battle was once a method available in British law for deciding legal cases. It was only abolished in 1819, as a result of a high-profile English murder case. Although the accused had been found not guilty, the victim's brother appealed. The accused offered to settle the issue through trial by battle, but the brother refused to fight him, so the accused walked free. The public was scandalized, and this legal option was eliminated in Britain – and, as a result of the union that existed between them at the time, in Ireland too.

Ireland had had its own notorious trial by battle case a few years before. In 1815, a farm labourer named Thomas Clancy shot retired naval Captain Bryan O'Reilly with a pistol, at close range, in broad daylight, in front of several witnesses on a road near Mullingar. O'Reilly lingered in agony for half an hour before he died.

Clancy was immediately caught and brought before Westmeath Magistrate John Charles Lyons. He made a full confession, declaring that he had been hired to commit the murder by a tenant of Margaret Talbot of Malahide Castle, who was considerably in arrears in rent. O'Reilly, a relative of Talbot's, acted as her land agent. Clancy had been paid 10 guineas in advance and promised thirty guineas as soon as the murder was carried out. Lyons had this confession drawn up as a deposition and signed and sworn to by the murderer.

Clancy was brought to trial at the Mullingar summer assizes a short while later. As the prosecution believed Clancy's confession was all the evidence they needed for a conviction, they did not call on any of the witnesses to testify. When the trial began, the defence got the confession thrown out on a technicality. The prosecution then asked for time to round up the witnesses to the crime and get them to court to testify, but the judge declined to allow any delay, as the jury had already been empanelled. Without any of this evidence against him, Clancy was acquitted.

O'Reilly's brother appealed the verdict to the Court of King's bench. After much legal discussion and several adjournments, Clancy, at his defence counsel's urging, offered the dead man's brother trial by battle. Chief Justice Downes was horrified by this turn of events.

'Can it be possible,' he exclaimed, 'that this "wager of battle" is seriously insisted on? Am I to understand this monstrous proposition as being propounded by the bar – that we, the judges of the Court of King's Bench – the recognised conservators of the public peace, are to become not merely the spectators, but the abettors of a mortal combat? Is that what you require of us?'

The matter was due to be heard in court in Dublin in November 1817, but a compromise was agreed between the two sides that put an end to the long-running farrago. Clancy withdrew his claim for trial by battle, pleaded guilty to the murder and was transported to Australia in order to save his life. At least that was the state of affairs as reported by a newspaper in November 1817.

Another reputable source recorded that the court continued to postpone judgment of the issue for so long that the act abolishing trial by battle was passed and came into force. On 24 August 1819, the court, having read the act, ordered Clancy discharged.

Full Circle

Today Stepaside is a commuter suburb of Dublin, but in 1893 it was a sleepy village. It was the unlikely location for a horrific murder that shocked the local population. Early on the morning of 21 May 1893, the body of a man who had been violently murdered was discovered. The man had been stunned by a blow to the head and then dragged unconscious across the road. It was clear from the blood-spattered scene that he had come-to at that stage and fought for his life. His body lay spread-eagled on its back, in a gateway to a field, with its head smashed in. Brain matter and blood was everywhere.

Despite the disfigured face, the dead man was quickly identified as an insurance agent named Bernard Cox who lived nearby. It was a difficult crime scene as heavy rain had fallen during the night, making it impossible to make casts of any footprints. Police feared that valuable evidence had been lost, but when the body was lifted for removal, an iron bar about two feet long was found beneath it. Someone had rifled through the dead man's pockets and various small coins had been flung away. Cox's umbrella, pipe, tobacco pouch and purse were missing.

Detective Bernard Casey later wrote an account of the investigation and recorded that one of his constables had quickly found out that the driver of a vehicle transporting porter from Blackrock had been seen talking to Bernard Cox at about 8pm the night of 20 May near the scene of the murder. Detective Casey journeyed to Blackrock and went to the pub whose porter van had been in Stepaside. 'The landlord immediately sent for the driver,' he later wrote. 'He told me that he had indeed met a man on the Saturday night, and that he had fitted the description of the victim. He also said that a bread van driver had stopped to talk to Cox.'

This bread van driver's name was John Brack and he lived at Golden Ball, a village only a mile away from Stepaside. Casey asked where he could find Brack and was told he usually spent his Sundays in Bray. Detective Casey was soon on his way by express train to Bray, where he hunted about for the man but was unable to find him. Giving up the search, he hurried back to the station to catch a train home, but he found that the last one had gone some time earlier. Luckily, Casey bargained with the driver of a jaunting car to take him home by road. While he was making the deal he overheard a man asking a uniformed policeman nearby how he could get home to Golden Ball as he had missed the train.

'I helpfully butted in,' wrote Casey, 'saying that as I was going to pass by Golden Ball I would be glad to give him a seat in the car. He thanked me, got in and we drove away. I introduced the subject of the murder and then he told me that he had seen me by the body in the morning. He said he'd gone away when he heard me asking questions. I pressed him on this and he nervously told me that he was not going to turn informer. After some gentle persuasion, though, he admitted he was Brack – the very man I had gone to Bray to find!'

Brack admitted that he had spoken to Cox at about 8.30pm the previous evening, but said the deceased had later been joined by one James Reilly. The pair had then disappeared from his view around a curve in the road. Casey paid off the jaunting car driver at Golden Ball and went on foot to the house where Brack and Reilly lodged. It was now about 1am on 22 May but Casey didn't have far to go. He knocked at the door and the owner opened it. Reilly, he was told, was asleep in the back room.

'I went through the kitchen and found him lying on the earthen floor with his coat and a sack over him,' Casey recalled. 'His head lay on the strangest pillow I have ever seen – a block of stone! Reilly got up quickly when he saw the policeman standing over him holding a candle. When Casey charged him with the murder and cautioned him, Reilly did not say a word. The detective noticed that his boots appeared to have been recently washed, but still there were dark stains on them that looked like blood. (Analysis would later confirm that this was, in fact, blood.) Casey borrowed a pair of boots from the landlord for Reilly to wear and seized his as evidence. With his prisoner walking in front of him, Casey set out into the night at 1.30am for the Stepaside police station.

'It would be impossible to describe my feelings as we walked along, the murderer and myself, in the stillness of the night towards the spot where the crime had been committed.' He later recalled. 'Along the road scarcely thirty hours before Cox had walked, to the spot where the man by my side mercilessly killed him. I must confess to a feeling of fear, a supernatural fear, quite apart from any apprehension I may have had about my own safety.

'The night was dark and somewhat stormy. Black clouds rolled over the hills about us and the trees and young groves were tossed about, the wind whistling hollowly through them. The moon was half gone and only a few stars were visible. Sombre gloom surrounded everything; a deep veil of clouds overhung the whole horizon.'

As they neared the blood-spattered site of the murder, Casey's nervousness increased. He dropped a pace behind his man and gripped his revolver more tightly. 'An appalling sense of loneliness took possession of me as we neared the leafy arch beneath which Bernard Cox's life had been cruelly battered out.' Reilly walked steadily on, with his head bent slightly forward.

Casey kept a tight hold of the revolver in his pocket, with the muzzle pointing directly at the middle of the prisoner's back. He was ready to pull the trigger at the first sign of Reilly trying to escape. 'Nearing fatal spot I wanted to see how the prisoner would behave,' he wrote. '[...] on arriving within 15 or 20 yards of the gateway where the death struggle had taken place, I once more drew the hammer to full cock.' The click made Reilly start, which in turn made the nervous policeman step back a pace and raise the gun to cover the prisoner. Reilly glanced round at him, then bent his head forward and walked on faster than before.

'A dozen steps brought us to the exact place and I could see the murdered man's blood,' Casey noted. 'Reilly looked quickly to the side where the gateway was, hesitated for a fraction of a second and then, throwing his head still further forward and lower down, he strolled on at such a pace that I had some difficulty in keeping up with him. "Easy, my man", I said, "we have plenty of time before us", and he immediately dropped back into his original stride.' They walked on for some time

James Reilly is taken to the police station in the middle of the night.

and the detective was relieved when they reached the paved street of Stepaside. 'A few minutes later, I had my prisoner safely in the strong-room and I seated myself, with immense relief, behind a stiff glass of whiskey by the barrack fire.'

James Reilly was brought before the magistrates at Dundrum petty sessions and remanded for a week to allow police to gather evidence. He was later charged with Bernard Cox's murder and committed for trial. Further searches uncovered Cox's missing umbrella and tobacco pouch nearby the murder scene. Good police work established a strong circumstantial case against Reilly. He appeared before Lord Chief Justice Sir Peter O'Brien on 2 August 1893.

The court was told that Bernard Cox and his wife resided at Stepaside. The victim made his living as an insurance agent and was well liked. Cox was a mild-mannered and kindly man, who often payed the arrears of monthly premiums out of his own pocket for people who did not have the money at the time, so they would not suffer financial penalties. Reilly often begged money and tobacco from Cox and the generous man never refused him. Cox often walked to Enniskerry and other places to conduct business.

The prosecutor said Reilly believed Cox was coming home with a large sum of money after a day's work and laid in wait to kill and rob him. He would have been disappointed as Cox had only a few coins on him. The court heard that Cox had arrived at Golden Ball at 7pm and was persuaded by a friend to have a drink in the local public house. He had a small whiskey and then went on his way home, meeting the driver of the porter van, then John Brack and finally James Reilly. After that nobody saw him alive.

Several witnesses testified that Reilly had kept to himself that day and was seen sitting on the wall that ran down the road where the body was found. A man who was casually employed in the neighbourhood stated that he saw Reilly on the afternoon of 20 May with an iron bar partly concealed up his sleeve.

Reilly's landlady testified that she and her husband were at supper at about 9.30pm on the evening of 20 May when he burst in through the door looking so pale and frightened that she asked him if he had seen a ghost. He made no reply, but went straight to his room.

The jury quickly found Reilly guilty and sentenced him to death at Kilmainham Gaol. The jail is now a museum, and its historic register records that Reilly was '5 foot 1 with black-grey hair, grey eyes and a fresh complexion. His right leg was short and he had scars on his hips.'

On 2 September Reilly's life came full circle when he was hanged at Kilmainham Gaol. He had been born within its walls thirty-five years earlier while his mother was serving a sentence for theft. Now he drew his last breath in the place where he had first seen the light of day.

Death at the Altar

The wedding day of Thomas Thompson and Fanny Jane Moffat at Knocknamuckley Church in County Armagh on 2 March 1888 was memorable for all the wrong reasons. Instead of being a joyful occasion it was a scene of terrible tragedy and heartbreak.

The 25-year-old bridegroom was a master spinner from the nearby town of Gifford. He was a widower, his first wife having died the year before. His bride was a farmer's daughter from nearby Lisnamintry village.

On the day of their wedding, the sexton's daughter, Elizabeth McCredy, unlocked the church shortly before 10am. The rector, Rev. Oates, arrived to conduct the wedding, and he was soon followed by William Thompson, the brother of Thomas Thompson's first wife, who walked in and sat in the fourth pew from the door on the left-hand side. The wedding party arrived a few minutes later.

Thompson and a bridesmaid were first to enter the church, followed by the bride and a groomsman, followed by another groomsman and a bridesmaid. As the bridegroom passed the pew where his brother-in-law was sitting, William Thompson stood up, calmly took a gun from his pocket and fired it into Thomas's back. The bullet penetrated his left lung, but the injured man managed to turn and grapple with his assailant.

Thomas Thompson shot on his wedding day.

William Thompson was forced to the ground by the two groomsmen, who managed to subdue and disarm him. Thomas Thompson was carried to the sexton's house beside the church, while one of the wedding party set off on horseback to Portadown for a doctor and the police. William Thompson was held in the graveyard, but made no attempt to escape.

Two doctors arrived and attended the wounded man. They quickly extracted the bullet from Thomas's lung and did their best for him. The police came with the doctors and arrested

William Thompson, charging him with attempted murder. Despite his serious injury, Thomas made a deposition. 'Oh, Will, I did not think you would do this to me. But I am dying, and I forgive you.' He died shortly afterwards and William was remanded in custody.

An inquest was held the following day and the court heard that William had told his brother-in-law he would shoot him if he ever remarried. He had told police that his sister had been Thomas's wife for only a year before she died, and that she had suffered from his poor treatment of her. Thomas had not attended her funeral, and William feared he would mistreat any other woman if he married again. William said he was also concerned for the future of the child his sister had with Thomas.

The shooting was described in detail and the jury could not fail to give the verdict that Thomas Thompson had died from a bullet wound inflicted by his brother-in-law. The jury added that there was not enough evidence to indicate whether William Thompson was of sound or unsound mind.

The trial took place at the Armagh assizes on 10 July 1888 and attracted a great deal of attention due to the extraordinary nature of the tragedy. The facts of the case were clear enough: William Thompson had bought a revolver and ammunition at a Portadown store the day before the wedding and used it to gun down Thomas Thompson. It only remained for the jury to decide if he was guilty of the charge of murder, which carried the sentence of death, or manslaughter. Thompson pleaded not guilty to the charge of murder, and his defence counsel, George Hill Smith, sought to claim it was a case of manslaughter.

James Orr prosecuted the case and said the facts were so plain that he did not wish to go into them in detail. In an ordinary murder case the jury must weigh the value of circumstantial evidence, but the murder of Thomas Thompson was carried out in front of a large number of witnesses. He reminded the jury that 'when a man committed an unlawful act without a proper excuse the law assumed that he had that malice which rendered him liable'. Several witnesses provided the court with testimony about the tragic events.

In William Thompson's defence, George Hill Smith claimed the prosecution had failed to prove that Thompson had a vindictive nature. He said he had never, during the course of his short professional career, been involved in a case that had moved him so deeply, or in which he had felt such a strong sympathy for the defendant.

Summing up the case, Mr Justice Murphy said there were no grounds to find the defendant guilty of manslaughter, which the defence had suggested, and that they should find him guilty of murder. 'The marriage of the deceased a second time might have occasioned some displeasure to the prisoner, but it did not furnish any excuse for the committal of any offence,' he said.

The only other verdict the jury could return was that the defendant had killed his brother-in-law while insane, but 'as he had told them before there was not a particle or thread of evidence to prove the defendant was of unsound mind when he committed the deed'.

The jury retired and then returned after ten minutes to find Thompson of murder.

Asked if he had anything to say before he was sentenced, Thompson replied:

Certainly, I have not anything to say why sentence of death should not be passed upon me. I have been guilty. I did it in a passion, but not with the motive that has been brought forward by the Crown – namely, that I wanted to prevent him marrying another. His marriage did not affect me at all, with the exception of this, that it brought up old memories which I could not overcome.

I have never tried to throw out that I was insane. I certainly was not in my proper mind for some time before I left work. I could not mind my work properly and I could not help thinking of old things that happened to my sister. I could not settle myself to do anything. I wanted to leave the country and get rid of old scenes altogether but my friends advised me to stop on account of my mother.

Every time that this man's name was mentioned I could not overcome my feelings. That was the reason why I wished to get rid of old scenes altogether. He was married to my sister and before the marriage he drew back and tried to disappoint her. He told many things to her which were not proper, and charged her with unfaithfulness towards him. Those things, I believe, were the cause of bringing the disease upon her, and the effect of this on her mind was the cause of her death.

I was greatly attached to her. She was my only sister and I could not overcome my feelings. It was impossible for me to overcome them, but certainly the idea of preventing him from marrying again never entered my mind [...]

Thompson said that seeing his sister's child reminded him how its mother had suffered with its father.

He [Thompson] passed up and down my door the day she died, and did not stop from his work. He never came to the funeral. I was at the expense of getting her medical assistance for a long time during her illness and was at the expense of the funeral, so that those things had a great effect upon my mind.

It was merely when I heard of the marriage and everything was brought up before me, when I thought of the way my sister had been treated, and when I believed that if she had not been married to this man, or if he had treated her as a wife, that she would be living today, that I felt overcome.

Thompson concluded his extraordinary speech saying that he had broken the law and deserved to die, but asked the judge for mercy. He remained calm as the judge sentenced him to death, then was led away. A few weeks later his death sentence was commuted to life imprisonment.

On a plea of insanity, Thompson was moved to Dundrum Criminal Lunatic Asylum in Dublin, from where he escaped a few weeks later and disappeared without trace. Eighteen years later, on 10 September 1906, he calmly walked into the police barracks at Markethill, County Armagh, and gave himself up. The author regrets to say he can find no further trace of Thompson in newspapers of the day.

A Tangled Web

Beautiful Broadstone Station was once the Dublin terminus of the Midland Great Western Railway. It was also the scene of a murder that fascinated people of that time. George Samuel Little was a well-liked cashier at Broadstone. On 13 November 1856, his young assistant William Chamberlain went home at 5pm, and Little worked late. He locked the office door after Chamberlain left and that was the last time he was seen alive.

At 7pm, Ann Gunning, who cleaned the offices in the evenings, went to Little's room and turned the handle. The door was locked, but the light was still on. Thinking Little was probably busy at work, she left him in peace. The door was still locked the next morning when Chamberlain arrived for work, and there was no response from inside. Chamberlain was wondering what to do next when one of Little's sisters arrived at the station looking for him. He had not returned home the previous night, and this was out of character.

Fearing that Little was lying ill inside his room, another railway employee, a carpenter called James Brophy, climbed onto the station roof and in through a window. He found Little lying dead on the floor, face down in a pool of blood. The office door was broken down and police were alerted. Little had been horribly murdered. He had received numerous injuries to the head from a small blunt instrument like a hammer, and his throat was cut. The killer must have stealthily crept up behind Little as he worked at his desk and attacked him.

How the killer had entered and left the office was never explained, but the key of the office was missing, suggesting the killer had walked out the door, locked it behind him and escaped. It seemed likely that the killer knew Little's routine and the premises well enough to escape through one of several exits without being seen. This suggested that the killer probably worked at the station. Although £1,600 was found untouched in Little's office, it was quickly established that £330 in notes, gold and silver coins was missing.

The last train departed Broadstone at 7.15pm, and after that the station lights were extinguished, leaving it in darkness. It is likely that the killer was still in the office when Ann Gunning tried the door, waiting to escape in the dark. Police questioned all those who worked at the station about their movements, but they made no progress in the investigation. A few weeks later, searchers found a small part of the missing money hidden in a water cistern at the station, but nothing else.

It was not until more than six months later, on 23 June 1857, that a woman came forward to the police and informed them that her husband, 43-year-old Englishman James Spollen, had killed George Little and stolen the money. Employed by the railway company as a painter and handyman, he lived with his wife and four children in one of the railway's cottages, near the station. Spollen had lost an eye in an accident and was described as balding, sandy-haired and whiskered. He had worked at the station for twelve years.

In a sworn statement, Mary Spollen declared that James had confessed to killing Little. On the night of the murder he had returned home across rooftops from Little's office at 8pm with a bucket full of gold and silver coins. Mary told police she had seen him burn Little's pocket-book and could prove her story was true by telling them where the rest of the stolen money was hidden.

The police eagerly accepted her offer, searched the places she told them to and found the money in two locations inside the terminal grounds. In a hole, gold, silver and notes were discovered in bags, inside a painter's tub, hidden under red lead used by painters. More money was discovered under a pile of stones. The weight of the stolen money was such that it was obvious that more than one person was involved in hiding it. Police suspected Spollen's 18-year-old son and namesake, but could not make a case against him.

Mary also claimed her husband came home that night with blood on some of his clothes. She said she burnt some of them, but that Spollen had just painted over other bloodstains on other items. Their home was searched but nothing was discovered. Spollen had been questioned along with other station workers after the murder, but had told police he had returned home after 5pm and had his supper. Afterwards, he had gone shopping with his wife at 6.30pm and they had returned home at 10.30pm. At the time his wife had verified this story.

When questioned again in June 1857, he repeated this story, but his wife, 10-year-old daughter Lucy and 14-year-old son Joseph claimed this was a lie. Lucy said he had returned home between 7 and 8pm. It was a moonlit night, she was looking out a window and she saw him use a ladder to climb onto the roof of an old forge nearby and lower something down the chimney. Joseph corroborated her story. With his closest family giving evidence against him, James Spollen was arrested on suspicion of the murder of George Little. A few days later, the missing key was discovered in a stream near the station where Mary Spollen said it would be.

A section of the Royal Canal near the station was drained and a razor with the name Spollen engraved on it was discovered almost immediately after a superintendent offered a guinea as a reward. It was clear it had not been in the canal when the search commenced as it was free of rust and corrosion. A hammer was discovered on the canal bed and this was most likely one of the murder weapons.

James Spollen's four day trial began on 7 August 1857 and at first it seemed the case against him was insurmountable, but it quickly became clear that it was not as solid as it seemed. The defence made much of the fact that Mary Spollen had originally told police they had both gone shopping on the evening of 13 November 1856. The court also heard that James Spollen had no idea his wife had given evidence against him until he had been brought before magistrates and she had called out, 'Confess your guilt, you unfortunate man! What I have done was to save your soul, and that you may repent of your crime!'

It seemed that the evidence against him was almost too good. Was he really so foolish as to cover the stolen money with the red lead he used at his job, or was he being framed by his wife and others? The prosecution said Spollen knew the station inside and out, but the judge pointed out that many other workers did too. Spollen had done work in Little's office, but witnesses were unclear about whether it had been around the time of the murder or some weeks before.

Because a wife could not testify against her husband in court, Mary Spollen was not put on the stand to give evidence – but her children were. It was this feature of the trial that made it so noteworthy. They calmly gave evidence against their father, but they never looked at him, their eyes remained firmly fixed on the table before them. As he listened to their testimony, James Spollen sobbed for a moment before mastering his emotions.

The defence attacked the weak points in the prosecution's case and the inconsistencies between the children's testimony and their original statements to the police. The defence suggested that the young children had been influenced by their mother to give damning testimony against their father, and the jury concurred. James Spollen was acquitted of the charge of murdering George Little.

When the verdict was read, a great cheer was heard from the crowds gathered outside the court, and sentiment inside was for Spollen too. But it is unclear whether this meant that they believed in his innocence or that they were merely shocked that a man could be condemned by his wife's accusations and testimony from his own young children, who may have been coached.

After hearing the 'not guilty' verdict, James Spollen was overcome with emotion and collapsed in tears, exclaiming 'My children, my children!' He was then seated and one of the turnkeys loosened his necktie and shirt collar, and gave him a drink of water. After he had recovered a little, Spollen dipped his handkerchief in water and bathed his face. He then stood and addressed the court.

My lords and gentlemen, my conviction was fixed that I stood before twelve of my countrymen with happy homes and they would impartially take my case into consideration, and they have done so. I have been brought here in a wrongful way —wrongfully by — I will not condemn the woman. I always liked the man, and I loved the woman, but it is a dreadful thing to be in the hands of a female tigress. I should return thanks to the two gentlemen, the pillars of the law, upon the bench. I may be too sensitive, perhaps, when I say the crown blackened my character too much. I have, however, escaped thanks be to God. My character, I am afraid, must remain triflingly impaired. If I can, I will retire to some colony, where I can eke out a trifling subsistence. I hope it will be in my power to do so.

James Spollen was discharged a free man, but his life was in ruins. He had lost his job and police prevented him from returning to Broadstone Station or to his own home. He sent a message to his wife saying that he bore her no ill-will, but police blocked its carrier from communicating with her.

A few days later, Spollen was arrested and charged with stealing the money, but the case was thrown out. He left Dublin and went to Liverpool and gave lectures about the murder case to raise some money. In January 1858, he sailed to Australia with his eldest son to make a new life.

Two Candles

Mary Clasby lived on North Gate Street in Athenry, County Galway, and she occasionally took in lodgers. In late November of 1901, her only one was Thomas Keeley, who had been staying with her for several weeks, since his arrival in the town. Reports described him as a 'cripple' suffering from poor health, who had been born in America and raised in Castlegrove, near Tuam, County Galway. Although a painter by trade, the 35-year-old was out of work and mostly begged for charity to get by.

A young boy from Newcastle named Richard Burns went into Athenry on the morning of 18 November and sold an ass and a cart-load of turf. A little after 10am, he was passing by 60-year-old Mary Clasby's house when he heard a man call him over. This person, who he did not see, asked the boy to buy him two candles and extended an arm out from behind a slightly open door holding two pence for him. Burns took the money from the man's hand and did as he was asked. When he returned, he put the candles into the same outstretched hand, then walked away.

A short while afterwards, a woman named Mary Seize called to the house with a delivery of milk. When she went into the kitchen she found Keeley sitting at the fire smoking a pipe. He told her Mary Clasby had a sore leg and was lying down and asked Seize to come back in the evening. She went to open the bedroom door, but when she put her hand on the latch Keeley pulled her away. After Mary Seize departed, Keeley was seen looking up and down the street.

Around midday, Delia Spelman called to the house to visit Mary. She entered and called out to her friend, but she received no reply. When she opened the bedroom door she saw a hand on the floor, became alarmed and ran for the police. Officers went to the house and found Mary Clasby lying there dead. Her knees were bent and her head was resting against the foot of the bedpost. She had serious head injuries and had clearly suffered a violent death. A bloodstained painter's hammer lay nearby and there were two lit candles about a yard from her feet.

At first there was no sign of her lodger, Thomas Keeley, who was the most obvious suspect, but the next day he was found in Tuam, nearly 20 miles away. When he was arrested, Keeley had a large amount of money and several items belonging to Mary Clasby in his possession.

On 20 November, a most unusual line-up took place in the Athenry police station. Instead of picking out a suspect from a group of men standing before him, Richard Burns was asked to pick out the right hand and arm of the man who had asked him to fetch the candles, from a choice of three stretched out from behind a door. The three hands were also shown to Burns holding the same type of candles he had bought. He also heard the three men speak.

Richard Burns identified one of the hands as resembling the one he had seen, and a coat sleeve as looking very like the one on the outstretched arm. He was also certain that one of the voices belonged to the man he had spoken with.

The hand and the voice the boy recognised in the line-up belonged to the same person – Thomas Keeley.

Keeley went on trial for Mary Clasby's murder on 24 March 1902 in Galway. He pleaded not guilty. The prosecution described how Keeley had arrived in Athenry several weeks before the murder and had become a familiar figure looking for odd jobs and begging on the streets. After witnesses testified about events on the morning of 18 November 1901, the prosecution said Thomas Keeley had been seen in a public house in Tuam at 7.30pm by a farmer called John Gormley, who knew him.

Keeley had offered him six pence, saying Gormley had stood to him before, but the farmer would not take the money. Instead, Keeley bought two bottles of stout and the men drank them. Keely also bought two pipes costing six pence and nine pence. He gave Gormley the cheaper pipe and bought tobacco for them to smoke. Gormley saw him take a bead case out of his pocket that contained ten sovereigns and pay the publican a half-sovereign.

Keeley then asked Gormley to join him in a room off the bar as he wanted to talk to him. In the room he handed Gormley a wad of money and asked him to count it for him. It amounted to £11 in notes. Keeley said he had earned it since he was last in Tuam in September. He asked Gormley to go with him to a local pawnbrokers and retrieve a suit he had pawned sometime before. There Keeley paid a sovereign, took the clothing back and got change. Afterwards they went to a public house next door and Keeley also bought two other men drinks.

When they left the public house, Gormley invited Keeley to stay the night at his farmhouse and Keely accepted. Keeley spent half a crown buying whiskey and a gallon of porter and they drank this with two other men. Keeley slept in the kitchen and was up before Gormley at 8am and offered to pay for his lodgings, but Gormley refused any money. Keeley complained of a sore heel, explaining that he had walked from Loughrea the day before. They went into the town again and had drinks in two public houses. Keeley also bought a razor, underwear, a vest, two pairs of socks and a necktie, and then the pair returned to Gormley's house around 2pm.

News of the murder had reached Tuam, and when a man named Thomas McGovern called into the house they talked about it. 'Is this not a great deed that has happened in Athenry,' McGovern commented as he smoked a pipe. 'A woman killed in Athenry and half the head cut off her with a hatchet.' Gormley noted that Keely looked stunned and then became agitated, alarming the others. The police were sent for and Sergeant Thomas Sheehy arrived on the farm shortly afterwards.

He asked Keeley to stand up so he could talk to him. 'I am going to ask you questions regarding the Athenry murder,' said the policeman and read him his rights. Keeley told him he had arrived in Tuam from Loughrea two days before, which Gormley knew was untrue. He also denied he had been in Athenry. Sergeant Sheehy arrested him for the murder of Mary Clasby and brought him back to the police station. Keeley was searched and found to have more than £19 on his person. Police also noted he had cuts on his shins that appeared to have been caused by kicks. A ring identified as Mary Clasby's was also found on him.

The court heard that a post-mortem examination of Mary Clasby's body carried out by Dr P.J. Quinlan at 6pm on the day of the murder found that she had five deep head wounds and estimated that she had died ten or twelve hours earlier. The jury also heard that Mary Clasby was quite well-off. After summing up the case, the judge concluded by noting that Keeley 'seemed to be a man not inclined to do his own work so long as he could get others to do it for him, and was offered employment and would not go to get it'.

He told the jury not to let any feeling influence the verdict, only to consider if Keeley committed the crime. He added that the prisoner was perfectly sane and although the lighting of two candles at the feet of his victim was peculiar, that did not make him mad. The jury found Keeley guilty but recommended mercy be shown to him. At that, many in court loudly expressed their horror and anger. Thomas Keeley was sentenced to be executed on 23 April 1902 and received no reprieve.

Two weeks after the trial, Keeley collapsed and was admitted to hospital. A tumour was found on his backbone and the condemned man underwent an operation to remove it, as they believed he would have died before his execution date. Although the operation was a success, Keeley's health was so poor that he was not expected to live longer than 23 April anyway. Returned to prison, Keeley admitted he had attacked Mary Clasby while she prayed.

There was no gallows at Galway Prison and a two-storey brick structure had to be quickly built against a wall there. On the second storey, an overhead beam with a rope hanging from it served as the scaffold over a hinged opening in the floor. The day before his execution, Keeley was clearly very ill and dying – he lapsed in and out of unconsciousness. On the day itself, the hangman pinioned him while he was unconscious. He woke up and was led to the execution house. Seeing the gallows, he panicked and the attending chaplain had to calm him down. The execution was carried out quickly, and Keeley became the last person to be executed at Galway Gaol.

A Family Affair

Thirty-year-old Patrick Dunne lived with his mother near Togher, a short distance from Daingean, County Offaly. The Shiel family lived on their farm nearby at Kilcoe. In 1869, a dispute arose between the two families over turf-cutting rights on a piece of land.

This bitterness spilled over into violence when Peter Shiel hit Patrick Dunne over the head with a spade. Shiel was later prosecuted for this vicious assault and sentenced to six months' imprisonment. This did not go down well with the Shiel family or Peter's sister Margaret – or Peggy, as she was known – was frequently heard threatening to kill Patrick Dunne in revenge – and that is what she did!

On 26 February 1870, Thomas Russell was returning to Daingean after 8pm accompanied by two friends, sisters Bridget and Julia Henry. They were a short distance from the town when they heard moaning nearby. Russell followed the sounds and discovered Paddy Dunne lying in a ditch near the roadside. 'Oh! I am killed!' exclaimed Dunne. He said he had been shot by Laurence and Peggy Shiel, had been lying in the ditch for half an hour and was cold and wet.

Russell went to help the wounded man and sent the sisters to Dunne's employer, John Ennis, for assistance. Help arrived a short while later, and the injured man was carefully carried into the town. Dr Henry Clarke attended Dunne and saw that he had been seriously injured. His head had eight wounds from shotgun pellets and a contused wound on his forehead and a cut on his throat inflicted by a knife. Despite his injuries, Dunne was fully alert and gave a clear account of what had happened.

Dunne was heading home after working on Ennis's farm and was met by Laurence and Peggy Shiel. They bid him good night and then shot him twice, beat him, cut his neck, threw him into the ditch and fled. Dunne believed he was dying and so did the doctor. He made a sworn statement in front of witnesses, and local justice of the peace Edmond Scully wrote it down. Dunne, who could not write, then affixed his mark to the document. His deposition reads:

> I, Patrick Dunne, of Togher, Daingean, do believe myself to be dying, and do declare that Peggy Shiel and Laurence Shiel were standing on the road at Togher, and on my way home the Saturday evening they bid me good night, when Peggy Shiel fired a shot at me. They both then went into Mr Ennis's field. I was afraid of them since the beginning of the turf.

Patrick Dunne passed away shortly after making the deposition. Witnesses later testified he was 'perfectly sensible and capable of making a statement'.

A warrant was issued for the arrests of the two Shiels. Police succeeded in arresting Peggy at her home, but her brother had fled. Peggy stated that she had been at home all evening with her father. She explained an injured hand by saying she had hurt it while lifting a sack of oats in the barn.

Police searched the murder scene that night by lamplight. Constable James Hazlett found a large pistol that had been recently fired and was broken. The next day, Constable James Brown found a knife nearby where Dunne had been found.

Constable Hazlett was sent in search of the wanted man and doggedly followed his trail. On the night of the murder, Laurence Shiel had made his way to Portarlington and taken the last train for Dublin. Some way up the line, Shiel got off the train in an effort to shake off pursuers, who he hoped would think he was heading for Dublin. He then doubled back, taking a train bound for Cork. Hazlett discovered the ruse, tracked the wanted man to Cork and arrested him while he waited to board a ship bound for America under the name Laurence Byrne.

Police discovered that Daingean blacksmith Michael Quinn had repaired a pistol for Laurence Shiel a few days before the murder, and Quinn identified the one police had found as the one he had fixed for a shilling. He said he had delivered the weapon to the Shiel farm, and that Peggy had been there and examined it. The Shiels had also shown him another pistol and asked if it had wanted repair, but he had said it was alright. Another tradesman in the town, Thomas Rooney, identified the knife police had found as one he had repaired for Laurence Shiel. An inquest was held two days after Patrick Dunne's murder. After deliberating for a short while, the jury returned a verdict of wilful murder against Laurence and Peggy Shiel.

They went on trial a few weeks later, on 1 April 1870, at the Tullamore courthouse. The evidence against 24-year-old Laurence and 29-year-old Peggy was damning. Patrick Dunne's dying declaration made a strong impression on those in the courtroom when it was read out, and witnesses testified that the dying man had been fully competent to make it. Dunne had repeatedly named the Shiels as his attackers. Testimony was heard from several witnesses placing Peggy and Laurence near the scene of the murder at the time it was committed that night.

Thomas Russell had met Laurence after 7pm when heading out from Daingean for his friend's house. George Baynham had met a woman and two men, one of whom was Laurence Shiel, on his way to Daingean near 8pm. He walked on, but heard the trio talking. He recalled the woman saying, 'He has to be here, and I don't see him here.' He met no one else and was just entering the town when he heard two shots coming from where he had met the people.

Other witnesses met Peggy and Laurence that evening around the same time and location. Another man heard the shots and witnessed a young man running towards the Shiels' house, but either could not or would not identify Laurence as the person. Evidence identifying the pistol and knife as belonging to the Shiels was heard, and a shopkeeper told the court he had sold them the shot. Newspapers used as wadding for the pistol discovered at the murder scene were matched to missing pages from a newspaper at the Shiel house.

Witnesses told the court that Peggy had frequently sworn to get even with Patrick Dunne. She was heard to say she would have him shot or do it herself. When her brother Peter had been sent to jail, Peggy had told Thomas Rooney she would have Dunne shot for £10. Rooney had told her to go to her priest and put such bad thoughts out of her head, and she had replied 'to hell with the priest'.

In her defence, Peggy's father Patrick swore she had not left the farm all day and that he would have known if she had. He said he had never seen the pistol before. A son of his had been shot and killed years before, and he never allowed his family to keep firearms 'lest the Devil might tempt them to revenge'. He also swore Peggy had injured her hand that day lifting a sack in the barn. The trial lasted two days, and in the end Laurence and Peggy were found guilty of the murder of Patrick Dunne and sentenced to death.

An appeal to commute their sentences failed. The lord lieutenant of Ireland was personally appealed to. His office made a full investigation of the case, but decided to let the law take its course. With no hope of a reprieve, the pair's demeanour changed and they became penitent and passed their time in prayer, resigned to their fate. The pair were hanged inside Tullamore Gaol on 7 May 1870 at 8am.

It was the first execution held behind closed doors since an 1868 act had abolished public executions. Peggy showed more composure on the scaffold than her brother, who looked anxious. When the trap door was pulled, both were killed instantly. Everyone present, including the black-hooded executioner, got down on their knees and prayed. The prison bell was rung and a black flag was run up on one of the front towers to show that the execution had taken place.

The bodies were kept suspended until the district coroner arrived at 12pm and held an inquest to determine the cause of death. The jury declared that brother and sister had been hanged, and added that their deaths had been barbaric and not in keeping with the 'requirements and spirit of this enlightened age'. They recommended that execution should be abolished, since there were ample other means of punishing criminals.

The Jealous Heart

Stephenstown House near the village of Knockbridge, County Louth was once the scene of a terrible murder-suicide. The tragedy took place on 7 October 1902, at which time the house was the residence of Major Matthew Fortescue. The victim was 26-year-old Alice Moore from Stradbally, County Waterford, who worked there as a maid. By all accounts she was a very pretty young woman – newspapers of the day described her as having a 'pre-possessing appearance'. The perpetrator was 45-year-old John Breen from Dublin, who was temporarily employed at the house as assistant butler.

The county coroner held an inquest the following day at Stephenstown House. Major Fortescue testified that he had employed Alice as a maid for the past eighteen months. She was warm and likeable and Mrs Fortescue thought of her as more of a friend than a servant. John Breen had been in his employ from October 1901 until April 1902, when he left the major's service to try his luck back in Dublin. He had returned to Stephenstown the previous week at the major's request to help out while he was entertaining a large party for the shooting season. It appeared that Alice Moore and John Breen had been engaged, but Alice had recently broken off the engagement. When he returned to the household he discovered that she was in a new relationship and was bitterly jealous and angry at his former lover.

Alice Moore is murdered.

Around 10.40pm, Major Fortescue and his guests were relaxing in the library when they heard the unmistakable sounds of three shots being fired in the dining room. They raced in and found Alice Moore and John Breen lying motionless on the floor. Breen was already dead, but Alice held on for a moment or two before fading away. A revolver lay near Breen, and the major recognised it as his own. He kept it in his dressing room unloaded, and kept the cartridges in the library and study. Breen would have known this and had permission to access all these rooms. Fortescue observed that the revolver had been fired three times.

John Bowers, the butler at Stephenstown, testified that he had been in the pantry at 7.30pm when Alice came in and asked his permission to wash her hands at the sink. Breen was at the other side of the sink when she came in and said he would not have such a woman beside him to wash her hands, and called her a lot of vile names. The footman John Smyth was there too and took offence at Breen's foul slurs against Alice.

Smyth had found a position in the household after Breen's departure in April and had become involved with Alice. He was furious with Breen and punched him several times. After trading blows with the younger man, Breen took up a knife and look like he was going to attack him, until Bowers jumped in between the pair and separated them. Bowers said Breen seemed 'queer and excited', but could not say if he had taken any drink. When asked when Breen might have got the revolver, Bowers guessed it must have been when the servants were at supper at 7pm, as Breen did not join them for the meal.

Major Fortescue and his guests had retired to the library at 10.30pm and some of the servants had then moved in to clear the dining room. Bowers was just outside the door, putting the good silverware back in the plate closet, when the three shots were fired. John Breen and Alice Moore were alone in the dining room, clearing the dining table. The gunshots followed each other in quick succession, with barely a second in between each one. The startled butler put down what he was holding, rushed in and saw the two lying on the ground. John Smyth ran in at the same time, and then left to get Major Fortescue. Bowers rushed to Alice and carefully lifted her head. She gave one sigh and died in his arms.

John Smyth was heard from next, and his testimony regarding the fracas in the pantry corroborated Bowers' evidence. Smyth admitted that he had being seeing Alice, but said he had not known Alice and Breen had been engaged.

Dr Flood then testified that he had reached the house at 12.30am and examined the bodies lying in the dining room. They lay about three yards apart, with their feet pointing towards each other and faces upwards. The doctor saw a large pool of blood under each head, and rigor mortis was setting in. The bullet had entered Alice's neck an inch and a half below her right ear and exited two inches below her left ear. The cause of her death was haemorrhage and shock.

Breen's lips were black and scorched and the corpse bled from the nose and mouth. He had shot himself through the head. A third bullet was lodged in the ceiling and Dr Flood concluded there must have been a brief struggle before Breen managed to shoot Alice. The jury returned a verdict, on the suggestion of the coroner, that Breen had shot Alice Moore in a fit of jealousy and then committed suicide.

Four days after she had been murdered, Alice Moore was laid to rest in the family plot in Stradbally Churchyard in County Waterford. A huge crowd attended the funeral to pay tribute to Alice and her family.

Cold Vengeance

In 1861, George Graham briefly employed John Logue at his farm in the townland of Ballymacbrennan, which lay between Lisburn and Saintfield in County Down. After only a few days, the teenager had taken a horse from a stable without permission and damaged a door. Graham struck Logue, the youth threatened him and Graham fired him.

Later that year, 17-year-old Logue was tried and convicted for stealing sheep from Graham's neighbour, James Wilson. Both Graham and Wilson were witnesses for the prosecution, and Logue was sentenced to four years' imprisonment. He spent this time at the notorious Spike Island in County Cork. Logue later described this as a training ground for criminals. Officials there said Logue was a dangerous convict, but a model student in the schoolroom. He was intelligent and composed verse on occasion.

Logue was released on 28 June 1865 and went to England. He committed a series of petty crimes, but was not caught and he returned in early July to his home district in County Down. For years he had sworn vengeance against those who had done him wrong, and now a small crime wave hit the area.

On 10 July, James Wilson's house was broken into and a gun, gunpowder and shot were taken, as well as a distinctive red handkerchief. The gun was found a few weeks later inside a haystack. On 13 July, a fire broke out in a yard belonging to another neighbour – some animals died and several haystacks were burnt. On 8 August, the home of Daniel Maguire was broken into and a gun, powder, a powder flask, percussion caps and a pair of silver sugar tongs were taken.

Then, in the early hours of 11 August, the Graham family were woken up by some knocking at the front door and someone shouting, 'Your pigs are on the road!' George Graham and his 10-year-old son Thomas got dressed quickly and went out to investigate. As George went outside, he saw a man standing in the shadows near the pigsty. At first he thought it was a neighbour, but when he saw the man pointing a gun at him George pushed his son back inside and made for safety himself.

The gunman fired and hit Thomas, who fell to the ground in agony. He had been hit in the lower spine. George Graham went to follow the fleeing gunman, but the man called out 'Stop, or I will give you the same sauce!' George had to retreat and see to Thomas, who told his father, 'Da, I'm living yet.' The family sought the help of neighbours and a doctor was called, but poor Thomas died a few hours later.

The grieving parents told police they had recognised the gunman as John Logue, and a hunt for the killer began. Several witnesses described seeing the same man over the next few hours. Logue remained in the area seeking work using the alias Shaw. He worked at the farm of the Moore family at Ballyleeson for a few days after the murder, but left without waiting for his wages. He must have thought the Moores were getting suspicious of him.

They noted that he was uneasy while there and often asked about the news and newspapers. 'Shaw' was heard to comment on the murder, saying that Logue was an 'awful fellow and a headstrong one'. One day at dinner the conversation turned to the murder and Shaw stated that Logue had intended to shoot the old man and not the son. They noted Shaw had a powder flask in his pocket and several papers of shot. When Shaw left their employment, he stole two shirts and a shearing hook.

Shaw had told them that the local minister, Rev. Maunsell, had once fined him seven shillings six pence for playing bullets on the road. A member of the Moore family asked Rev. Maunsell about this, and he recalled that he had actually fined John Logue. The Moore family noted that Shaw owned a pair of silver sugar tongs and a red handkerchief, allowing police to link Logue to the crimes that had occurred in the area before the murder.

Logue was said to have worked at saving hay on the Watters family's farm at Dundrod from 17 to 29 August. On 30 August, he showed up at the home of Magistrate Captain James Whitla at Lismoyle, near Dunmurry looking for work. He said his name was William Shaw and claimed to be from the Hillhall area. Captain Whitla was suspicious of the stranger and arrested him after realising he matched the description of the wanted man. Shaw was later identified as John Logue and jailed at Downpatrick Prison while he awaited trial. In his possession he was found to have buckles, percussion caps, powder, a red handkerchief, a knife and other items stolen in the robberies, which were identified by the owners.

John Logue stood trial for the murder of 10-year-old Thomas Graham at Downpatrick Courthouse on 15 March 1866. The prosecution's case was that George Graham and his wife had clearly seen the murderer on the bright, moonlit night of 11 August 1865. Graham had known Logue for years and recognised him immediately. When Logue had been jailed for stealing sheep, he had sworn vengeance against Graham. After he was released, Logue had stalked the Graham family for several nights and even hid in a nearby wood to observe the farm. He had stolen the family's dog in an effort to lure George out to look for it a few nights before. When these attempts to ambush and kill George Graham failed, he had decided on a more direct approach, which proved fatal to Thomas.

Despite the defence's best attempts, John Logue was found guilty of murdering Thomas Graham and sentenced to be publicly hanged on 19 April 1866 outside Downpatrick Prison. When asked by the judge if he had anything to say about why he should not be sentenced to death, Logue replied, 'I have nothing to say.' He seemed indifferent when the judge tearfully sentenced him to be executed.

On the day following his conviction, Logue broke down in tears, but his usual indifferent manner soon returned. Whether hopes of gaining a reprieve kept his spirits up is hard to say. A close watch was kept on the condemned prisoner. While awaiting trial, he had attempted to escape using a piece of pipe to dig through the walls of his cell. He had managed to loosen a few bricks before he was discovered. Several petitions were sent to the lord lieutenant of Ireland, asking him to spare Logue's life, but these only elicited the reply that the case had been fully considered and the lord lieutenant 'felt it his painful duty to leave the law to take its course'.

Logue was attended by a Methodist minister in the days before his execution and took comfort from prayer.

Although asked several times if he wished to unburden his conscience, Logue continued to claim he was innocent of the boy's murder. On the morning of his execution, Logue rose at 6.30am, breakfasted and then prayed with several clergy. Shortly before 8am he was brought by warders from his cell to the room near the scaffold. His arms were pinioned behind his back by the hangman and then he was led up to the scaffold. He was described as 'having absolute coolness, without a trace of either bravado or emotion' as he climbed up the steps to the scaffold.

The executioner, who was said to have been from Wexford, asked the condemned man if he had anything to say. 'No, no,' replied Logue, and the executioner pulled a hood over his face and moved him onto the trapdoor. He placed the knotted noose around Logue's neck and adjusted it. After a nod from the sheriff, the executioner pulled the bolt. A crowd of some 400 people – including women and children – had gathered to watch the execution, even though it was raining heavily. After an hour, the body was taken down and quietly buried in the grounds of the prison.

The Dancing Men

A little after 4pm on 8 August 1880, Thomas Boyd was being driven from his home, Chilcomb Lodge, to a farm he owned at Shanbogh, County Kilkenny, half a mile away and less than 2 miles from New Ross. With him were his sons Evans and Charles and his nephew Gladwell, who was holding the reins. He did this every Sunday and his routine would have been well known. Thomas and Gladwell sat on one side of the trap and Evans and Charles the other. As they neared the townland of Shanbogh, three men suddenly jumped out onto the road and began dancing about.

At first Thomas Boyd thought the men were mummers, as there was a tradition of mummers entertaining around harvest time. They were dressed from head to toe in canvas smocks and they also wore leggings, red masks and linen caps. Alarmingly, they carried rifles fixed with bayonets. Approaching the horse and trap, which had come to a near stop, the masked men pointed their weapons at the Boyds.

One attacker moved to Thomas and Gladwell's side while the other two went to the brothers. One bayonet came so close to Evans' face that it almost entered his mouth, but he knocked it away. As he did so the gun was fired and the bullet grazed his leg. The other two rifles were fired almost simultaneously. Gladwell deflected the

The Boyd family encounters masked gunmen.

rifled aimed at his uncle with his whip and Thomas only received a wound to his shoulder. Charles received a direct hit from his attacker.

A bullet entered the left side of his chest, under his heart, went through a lung and exited near his spine. This bullet then caused the minor wound to his father's shoulder. All this happened within a few seconds and Thomas grabbed the reins, whipping the horses away at top speed shouting, 'Murderers!' The attackers pursued the trap a short distance but could not keep up. Acting Constable Thomas Byrne heard the shots and cries and rushed out of his father-in-law's nearby cottage, but his wife clung to him, preventing him from following the attackers as they fled the scene. Gladwell jumped from the trap and ran through the fields to Chilcomb Lodge to raise the alarm, and Thomas Boyd's brothers, both doctors, were sent for. Charles died at 1.30am on 9 August.

Why had Thomas Boyd and his family been targeted? Boyd was a successful solicitor in New Ross and acted as an agent for several landlords. He was also Crown Prosecutor for Tipperary and Crown Solicitor for Kilkenny. He had also bought the Shanbogh estate some years previously and made himself unpopular by raising the rents. Five of the thirty tenants had refused to pay the increased rents and amongst these were several members of the Phelan family.

An hour after the shooting, police arrested brothers John and Walter Phelan after Evans Boyd identified them as two of the attackers. Several others were also arrested on suspicion of involvement in the shooting, bringing the number imprisoned for the murder in Kilkenny Gaol to eleven. While these people were incarcerated, hundreds of people from near and far helped save the suspects' harvests. Police searched the spot where the attackers had lain in wait and a brandy bottle and a whiskey bottle with a label from a Rosbercon public house were discovered. Nine of the suspects were released without charge, leaving only John and Walter Phelan to stand trial ten months later in Dublin on 27 June 1881. Walter was tried first and pleaded not guilty.

The prosecution told the court Boyd had bought Shanbogh estate and all the land was revalued. The accused men were brothers of one of the five tenants that refused to sign new leases. He claimed that Evans Boyd had recognised two if not three of the attackers despite their disguises. He was adamant he recognised Walter Phelan's voice, hearing him shout during the attack, 'Not one shot!' At their home, police found two caps similar to those used for the disguises and some cartridges and on their brother Richard's farm they found canvas similar to that worn by the attackers.

The crime had been committed in broad daylight and it would not have been attempted if the attackers had not been certain they could escape safely. The prosecution seemed to suggest there was a conspiracy in the locality. Four witnesses swore that John Phelan had been playing cards with them at the time of the murder. All of these had been suspected of involvement of the murder but were later released without charge. The chief prosecution witness against Walter Phelan was Evans Boyd. Neither Thomas nor Gladwell Boyd could identify the attackers. He explained he had known Walter for many years and recognised his voice. Evans also claimed it was John Phelan who shot his brother.

Under cross examination, Evans admitted that, when told the Phelans had been arrested, he had said, 'It is all no use. These are not the parties at all.' He explained, 'I had first asked, were they Phelans of the crossroads, and some of them said, "No, of the Churchyard," and I said that was wrong they were not the Phelans at all.' A local man testified that he had seen three men dressed in white fleeing the scene after the murder and none were Walter or John Phelan.

Acting Constable Byrne could not identify the men either as they were masked and in disguise. Hugh Mahon of the *Wexford People* and the *New Ross Standard* told the court he had been with Walter Phelan on the day of the shooting from 12am until between 3.30pm and 4pm before leaving Phelan's home at Shanbogh crossroads. Walter's sister testified that she saw three strange men dressed in white in the fields and heard the shots. Her brother had been half a mile away at the time looking at some horses.

The defence reminded the jury that Evans Boyd had identified John as his brother's killer yet Walter was now on trial. He reminded them that the police did not find the canvas in a shed until 31 August – weeks after the murder. If the Phelans were guilty they would hardly have left such evidence lying about. The defence claimed that Evans suffered from a spinal complaint which might have affected his judgement. If he was correct in naming John Phelan, then all those who said they were playing cards with him at the time of the murder were guilty of perjury.

The court also heard that when Evans heard who was arrested, he had said it was the wrong Phelans. Police also admitted that when the brothers had been arrested after the murder they had not been drinking, contrary to evidence that the attackers had left bottles of alcohol behind. The defence pointed out the canvas found on Richard Phelan's farm was found in an open shed, where anyone could have left it.

The prosecution rubbished the defence's claim that the attackers were strangers, pointing out that they clearly knew the area and the Boyds' movements. The canvas found on Richard's farm had been cut up to make the attacker's disguises. Walter Phelan had been placed near the murder at the time. Referring to the card players' alibi, the prosecution remarked how extraordinary it was that no one had got up when they heard the shooting. This was because they already knew and the card game was a sham alibi for John.

After less than an hour's deliberation, Walter Phelan was found not guilty. The brothers remained in custody as there were still charges pending over the shooting, but all remaining charges were dropped the following day and Walter and John were released. News of the verdict was warmly welcomed by the local populace, who lit tar barrels across the area in celebration. Walter Phelan's mental health suffered badly in prison and he was later admitted to Kilkenny Mental Asylum in 1883 and remained there until his death in 1944 at the age of 87.

Dark Water

At the end of May 1928, the Dublin Fire Brigade was drafted in to drain Falmore Quarry, which was only 3 miles from Dundalk, County Louth. The operation was part of the effort to find a missing woman who had lived nearby. By 1 June the fireman had spent four days emptying the quarry of over 4 million gallons of water. Their efforts were not in vain: a large sack containing human remains was discovered at the bottom of the nearly empty quarry.

The person had been dismembered and carefully stuffed into the sack. The state pathologist conducted a post-mortem examination of the remains and concluded the person had probably been strangled as a neck bone had been broken. Given the clean cuts on the corpse, the killer had some knowledge of butchery. Although the remains were badly decomposed, the body was identified as that of the missing woman, Mary Callan, through dental records. Clothing and shoes present were also identified as hers.

In May 1927, Father James McKeone was parish priest of Faughart, County Louth and resided in the parochial house in Balregan, close to Falmouth Quarry. He had two servants, 19-year-old Gerard Toal and 27-year-old Mary Callan. Toal, from Blackrock, County Louth, was orphaned at a young age and had fallen foul of the law.

At the age of 12, he had been convicted of robbery and had spent four years in Artane Industrial School in Dublin. Father McKeone had taken pity on the youth and given him a job as a general handyman and driver. Toal was described as only five feet four inches tall and dark haired and slightly built. He was also quite sullen and not very talkative.

Mary Callan had a far happier upbringing in Culloville, County Monaghan and was described as educated and religious. She was also very attractive. She was employed as the priest's housekeeper. It was well known that Mary and Gerard did not get on. In fact, despite working so closely they barely spoke to each other and ate their meals at different times or at different tables. It was clear they could not stand each other.

On 16 May 1927, Father McKeone had to go to Dublin. Mary served him his breakfast and Gerard drove him to the station to catch the 12pm train. As he departed, Mary was about to wash laundry. That was the last time he saw her alive. Gerard picked him up from the train station that night at 7.40pm. Father McKeone was puzzled when Mary was not in the house on his return, but assumed she had gone out.

When she did not return, he searched the house and saw many of her clothes were missing and the kitchen fire had gone out. When Gerard came in, Father McKeone suggested that maybe her mother was sick and she had gone to her. Gerard said she was dressed in her best clothes when he returned from the station that morning and had said she was going away. After dinner, she had gone upstairs and that was the last he had seen of her, as he had spent the day working in the garden before heading to pick up Father McKeone.

Her bicycle was missing and the laundry had not been finished. Father McKeone also noticed a small part of the kitchen floor looked as if it had been thoroughly scrubbed. The next day, the priest sent Gerard to her mother's house in Cullovile, 8 miles away, to see if Mary was there. While Toal was gone, Father McKeone called on a friend of Mary's, Peggy Gallagher, but she could shed no light on her disappearance.

He had her look and see what was missing from Mary's room. Peggy noticed Mary's best shoes were still there, as was her suitcase. Present also was Mary's Bible, her Child of Mary medal and rosary beads. Peggy knew Mary never went anywhere without the medal and beads and was alarmed. References from previous employers were also found in the room. It made no sense.

When Gerard returned, he said Mary had not been at her mother's. He added that there had been something wrong with her when she went away. Later he explained that sometimes he found her acting strangely, talking to herself and waving her arms and hands about. Despite being alarmed at Mary's puzzling disappearance, Father McKeone waited for a few days before reporting her missing. Gardaí did nothing about the missing woman. They did not make any enquiries or issue any description to the press of Mary Callan.

They only arrived at the parochial house on 30 May to question Father McKeone, Toal and Peggy, who had now taken up Mary's job. Before leaving, they said they would return the following day to search the area. That night, Peggy saw a fire lit where Gerard slept in an outhouse and Father McKeone investigated and found he was burning papers. The next day, he saw Gerard burning clothes in a nearby field but thought nothing of it. Father McKeone may not have suspected Toal was involved in Mary's disappearance, but Peggy was certain of it.

When Toal left his room unlocked, she would search it. She found a prayer book in his room similar to the one Mary had, but the page on which she had written her name on had been torn out and Toal had written his name on the next page. Father McKeone found a blanket in the outhouse, and Peggy was certain it had been Mary's. Despite finding mounting circumstantial evidence that Toal had been involved in Mary's disappearance, Father McKeone did nothing until Peggy persuaded him to search Toal's room again on 24 March.

He found parts of a bicycle, a watch and ladies dress cords. When Toal returned, Father McKeone questioned him about his findings and was not satisfied by the answers he got. When he told Toal he suspected him of being involved in Mary's disappearance, Gerard replied that he knew nothing about it. The next day, Gerard said he had bought the parts from a man named Halfpenny in Blackrock. Father McKeone drove there with Toal and found the man had emigrated a year before. Toal then changed his story and said he had burgled a shop in Dundalk. Gardaí would later establish that this was untrue.

When they returned to the parochial house, Peggy identified the watch the priest had found as Mary's and the bicycle parts looked similar to those on Mary's bike. He drove Toal to the garda station in Dundalk and told them that he believed the youth had killed his housekeeper. A few hours later the gardaí returned with Toal and searched the property. To Peggy and Father McKeone's astonishment, they left Toal at the house, having found he had no case to answer.

On 7 April, Toal left Balregan, telling Father McKeone he was going to his uncle's in Belfast and was planning to emigrate to Canada. It is not clear whether he had been fired or left on his own accord. The following day, gardaí arrived at the parochial house to question Toal about the theft of a suit from a Dundalk draper shop. Toal was quickly arrested and brought back to Dundalk prison while he awaited trial for the theft.

It was only at this stage that wiser heads in the force began to question Toal about Mary Callan's disappearance. Chillingly, he admitted climbing a ladder to look into her room while she was getting ready to go to bed. On 7 May, experienced Detective Superintendent Hunt took over the case of Mary Callan's disappearance. He suspected Toal from the start and ordered an extensive search of the Balregan property. The search turned up several items that Peggy identified as belonging to Mary Callan, but Toal could not identify the items. As Falmouth Quarry was only a short distance from the priest's house, Superintendent Hunt realised it was an obvious location to dump a body and had it drained.

After the discovery of her body, Toal was charged with the murder of Mary Callan and stood trial on 23 July 1928. Although the case against Gerard Toal was largely circumstantial, it was compelling and he was found guilty and sentenced to death. He was executed on 23 August 1928 and died without admitting he had killed Mary Callan.

The Mespil Road Mystery

There was no doubt that John Stokes had been murdered by his brother-in-law, Leo O'Brien. The real mystery was: what had been his motive? And why had the deceased man's family tried to prevent it becoming known?

Just after 6.30pm on 3 November 1934, gardaí in Dublin received a phone call reporting a shooting at 33 Mespil Road. Widower Bridget Marie lived there with an unmarried daughter, Maureen. Another daughter, Gabriel, lived upstairs in a flat with her husband John Stokes and their 5-year-old son, Louis. Arriving at the house, detectives found 38-year-old Stokes, a civil servant, lying dead. Mrs Marie told them he had been shot by her other son-in-law, Commandant Leo O'Brien, who had then calmly left and cycled in the direction of his home at Beggar's Bush Barracks, half a mile away.

Mrs Marie said that O'Brien had knocked at her door at 6.30pm and asked if Jack – John Stokes – was in. O'Brien was wearing civilian clothes and an overcoat. Mrs Marie, who had not seen O'Brien, replied 'Yes' and ushered him into the sitting room while she called Stokes downstairs. John Stokes came into the sitting room and walked over to the fire and stood with his back to it. Commandant O'Brien stood opposite him at the other side of the table.

Mrs Marie came into the room, and as she walked across to the window, she noticed a revolver lying on the table near Stokes. 'What in God's name is that?' she exclaimed and shuddered when John Stokes replied that it was a real revolver. Gabriel Stokes then came into the room and stood beside her husband at the fireplace. Maureen entered the room as well and a maid was also present in the house.

The two men were speaking sharply to each other. Stokes said, 'Well Leo, up to last night I held my tongue,' and O'Brien replied, 'You have finished my life with Leonie, I am going to finish yours now.' He pulled a gun from his pocket and shot Stokes three times. John Stokes cried out, 'Oh, my God,' and tried to struggle across the room, but collapsed and died. While this was happening, Louis came into the room and Maureen quickly brought him out.

The four women present in the house were shocked, but O'Brien remained calm. He put his gun back in his pocket and went to leave. The women tried to stop him, but he said that he was going to give himself up to the police and left the house before riding away in the direction of Beggar's Bush.

The Guards arrived at the barracks at 7.10pm and O'Brien walked out to meet them and confirmed his identity. They told him he was being arrested for the murder of John Stokes and he replied, 'Right, oh.' He asked, 'Is he dead?' A detective said yes and O'Brien said, 'He deserved it damn well right.' Detectives learned that 34-year-old O'Brien had actively served with the IRA and joined the Irish Army after 1922, when the Free State was established.

He pleaded not guilty when he stood trial at the Central Criminal Court in Dublin on 19 March 1935. The prosecution outlined the events on 3 November 1934 and contended that the gun on the table had been placed there by O'Brien for the purpose of inducing Stokes to defend himself. Although it was loaded, there was no cartridge in the breach, so if Stokes had taken it up it would not have fired – in sharp contrast to O'Brien's fully loaded weapon.

Mrs Marie told the court that O'Brien's wife, her daughter Leonie, had visited her for twenty minutes at 5.40pm then related to the court the terrible event that followed. The next witness was Gabriel Stokes, who corroborated her mother's testimony, adding that her husband warned her not to touch the gun saying, 'Don't touch it, it is real, and I want you and your mother to be witnesses.' Under cross-examination she admitted that the two families had been on good terms until several weeks before, when a coolness developed in their friendship.

On the face of it, the defence had an uphill struggle, but they mounted a strong case. They did not dispute O'Brien shooting Stokes, but asked the jury to consider his mental state when he had killed his brother-in-law. Their case was that O'Brien was so unbalanced at the time of the shooting that he was unaware of what he had done.

The defence went on to say that the families had been on good terms until about two months before the shooting, but had become estranged when Louis had spent an afternoon at the barracks but was sent home without getting his tea. Afterwards, the families had met and discussed the incident and Stokes had make a remark about O'Brien winning money betting on dog racing.

Relations had further soured when Gabriel called to the barracks with two lady friends but were not admitted by her sister, Leonie, as she was not prepared at that time to entertain strangers. No slight had been intended by Leonie O'Brien. She had called to her mother's house on 3 November 1934 to explain this and returned home shortly after 6pm. Her husband had remained home to look after their infant daughter.

When she returned she asked her husband, 'Is it true that you have been going with other women and giving them expensive presents?' O'Brien denied this accusation and his wife added that, 'Jack said so.' The defence said that this terrible accusation shattered Leo O'Brien and unhinged him. Up till this point O'Brien's motive had remained unknown, while his relatives were happy to imply he had killed Stokes over trivial disputes. The defence suggested that O'Brien's military training had allowed him to act in a quiet, steady manner on the night of the killing. During his active service with the IRA he had lived under constant strain for years and the defence claimed this might well have contributed to his poor mental health.

Leo O'Brien took the stand and gave evidence on his defence. He claimed to remember nothing from the night of 3 November. Referring to the financial pressure he had been under, O'Brien explained he had an overdraft of £60 and instead of deducting £10 from his monthly wages of £41, the bank unreasonably retained all of his wages. Faced with severe financial embarrassment, O'Brien had tendered his resignation, but a friend had lent him £100 and he had withdrawn his resignation.

Describing what had provoked the killing of his brother-in-law, he said his wife had accused him of being unfaithful and asked him if he knew of a girl who visited the house next to 33 Mespil Road. He said she had seen the girl going to the house and had been introduced to her sometime previously, adding that the girl had been with a gentleman he knew from a dance.

He asked her who had said all this about him and his wife said that when she had called to her mother's house, the first thing her mother had said to her was that she never thought she would see the day when her daughter would turn her own sister away from her door, because of that blackguard in Beggar's Bush Barracks, who was going around with other women and buying them presents to the neglect of his wife and child.

Hearing this, O'Brien became very angry and asked her who had said all this. His wife replied, 'Jack has said so – and he knows all about it.' O'Brien told his wife it was all untrue, but she stormed out of the room, saying, 'That is how you are £200 in debt.' O'Brien told the court he had no clear memory of what happened after his wife left. The next thing he remembered was finding himself at the Garda station.

Dr Richard Leeper of St Patrick's Hospital testified that O'Brien was suffering from exophthalmic goitre and symptoms of Grave's disease, characterised by an agitated melancholic state, paranoia and prone to obsessions which could lead to acts of violence. He added that O'Brien was neurotic. Dr Leeper added that he had never come across such an amazing case in his forty years' experience. A Dr John Fitzgerald from Grangegorman Mental Hospital testified that he found O'Brien neurotic and mentally unstable and that he might have forgotten what had happened due to shock.

A doctor for the prosecution found O'Brien perfectly sane, but admitted under cross-examination that a mental shock could produce temporary insanity. The defence's case concluded that O'Brien had been normal before the shooting but had been temporarily driven insane by his wife's accusation of infidelity. The prosecution held that he had shot Stokes out of hatred without any regard to the consequences. Summing up, the judge pointed out that doctors had been prevented from examining O'Brien for over a week after the shooting. After three hours' deliberation, the jury were unable to deliver a verdict and were discharged.

A retrial took place on 24 June 1935. Again the issue of Leo O'Brien's sanity at the time of the murder was argued. This time, the jury found him guilty of murder, but added recommendation to mercy. O'Brien was sentenced to death and an appeal against the verdict was dismissed a month later. With his execution scheduled for 14 August 1935, Leo O'Brien learned on 9 August that his death sentence was commuted to life imprisonment. After he had been sentenced to death, a massive campaign had gathered nearly 60,000 signatures on a petition for a reprieve. Many public figures, including bishops, had added their support. Leo O'Brien was released from prison in 1947 after serving twelve years for the murder.

Sanctuary

William Cousins lived on a small farm near Killinick, County Wexford. His wife died in 1920, leaving him with their 20-year-old son John. These two men were soon joined on the farm by William's sister Jane, her husband Andrew O'Brien and their son. The O'Briens sold their cottage, invested the proceeds in William's farm and moved into the impressive two-storey thatched farmhouse, which was called Sanctuary and dated from the seventeenth century.

The arrangement seemed to suit all parties, but in 1929 Andrew O'Brien deserted his wife and son and disappeared to England. This left Jane in a vulnerable position, as she had no right of residence and could be asked to move out at any time. After investing in Sanctuary and working there for years, she could be left with nothing.

When John Cousins got engaged in 1931 to a neighbour's daughter, Annie McGuire, Jane feared the worst. Then William died and the property passed to his son, all of which delayed the wedding until June 1932. Jane knew she would have to move out by then.

Jane made little secret of her animosity towards Annie, and secretly sent her anonymous postcards with rude messages. John and Annie thought them odd but funny and told no one about them except for the local garda. One day,

Annie went to the post office and saw Jane chatting with the postmistress. As Annie came in, Jane went to leave, saying, 'I'd better run now or Annie'll think I'm the one who's sending those letters.' Jane's remark inadvertently confirmed Annie's suspicions.

We don't know how long Jane planned to kill her nephew, but two weeks before the murder unknown persons posted 'Informers Beware! IRA' on the roadside outside the house. John Cousins had actively campaigned for the Cumann na nGaedheal party for the elections on 9 March, angering the IRA. Jane posted the anonymous signs and set in motion her plan to blame the IRA for her nephew's murder. John had a gun illegally hidden in the house and she decided to kill him with it.

On 25 March 1932 a neighbour saw Jane cutting a hole in the whitethorn hedge that lined the driveway. She picked a spot just inside the gate that gave her a clear line of sight on anyone coming up the driveway. She even repainted the gateposts with a fresh coat of white a few days before. The McGuires threw a party on 26 March to celebrate their daughter's impending marriage. John O'Brien was invited, but politely declined preferring instead to go to the cinema with his girlfriend in Wexford that evening.

That night, Jane O'Brien lay in wait behind the hedge for her nephew to return from the McGuires', the shotgun sticking through the hole she had cut. Sometime after 11.30pm she would have heard him leaving the house down the road, walking towards his home and then saying good night to his friend Jemmy O'Reilly at the gate. As John Cousins passed in front of the gatepost, Jane fired. Jemmy heard the shot and rushed back, finding his friend doubled over.

Thinking Sanctuary was not a safe place to bring the wounded man, Jemmy dragged him away to the closest house. The local priest, doctor and the gardaí were called. They arrived on the scene before 1am and found the wounded man lying outside in the cold and rain, where Jemmy had left him to fetch help. Why the injured man was left outside instead of being brought indoors is a mystery. John Cousins lay in agony for an hour and a half before a car set out to bring him the short distance to the county hospital in Wexford town. By the time the car arrived there he was dead.

In the early hours of 27 March, gardaí arrived at Sanctuary with John O'Brien to inform Jane of her nephew's death. The house was in darkness and Jane opened the door to them in her nightdress, holding a candle. Sergeant Hanley noticed that she began to 'whimper or sob', although she did not cry. As far as he knew, nobody had told Jane that her nephew had been shot, and he was suspicious. Furthermore, when Sergeant Hanley said her nephew John had had an accident, Jane asked if it was a motor accident. Sergeant Hanley did not answer and Jane did not enquire about the nature of John's injuries, which would have been the natural thing to do. Nor did she ask to see him.

As the gardaí went to depart, John O'Brien panicked, afraid his cousin's killers would strike again. He believed John had been shot by the IRA. He rushed to one garda and flung his arms around the man's neck.

'Don't go!' he pleaded. 'Leave somebody with us.'

'Have sense, John,' Sergeant Hanley snapped. 'Don't be frightening your mother.'

The guards decided to stay a little longer and asked to search John Cousins' room for clues. Before they left they posted an officer at the gate, to John O'Brien's relief.

The gardaí returned at first light to make a proper search. Sergeant Hanley found a wad and cartridge case just inside the gate. Pellets embedded in a gatepost allowed them to determine the point of origin of the gunshot. They found the hole in the hedge that Jane had cut, and the spot behind it where she had waited.

Even though the earth had been softened by rain, there were no tracks in the field to suggest that the murderer had fled away from Sanctuary. Clearly, the person had gone in the direction of the house. A gap in the hedge near the house showed signs that someone had used it and seemed to confirm this theory.

Chief Superintendent McCarthy arrived on the scene at 8am and was briefed on the discoveries. He asked John O'Brien if there was a handsaw on the property, and John produced one from a shed. It was clear it had been recently used, as wood shavings clung to its teeth. Mother and son denied having used it or having any knowledge of John Cousins using it.

Superintendent McCarthy interviewed Jane. She told him the previous evening had been a normal one and denied there was animosity between herself and her nephew. McCarthy did not believe her and told Jane he suspected that she had killed John and the gun was concealed in the house. She denied knowing anything about the murder and told McCarthy to search the house again. He did just that, but first he sent Jane to her room while his men searched the other rooms first.

When they got to the room, the guard escorting Jane noticed she had a cut on her hand and asked how she had got it. 'It may have been the cat or the dog but at any rate it was not the bush,' she said, oddly. Superintendent McCarthy left her room till last to search as he believed the gun was probably there and wanted to pile the pressure on Jane.

Entering the room, he bluffed and told her he knew the gun was there and asked her to hand it over and save them having to search for it. She denied all knowledge of a gun, but Superintendent McCarthy continued to pile on pressure by saying he knew who cut the bush in the driveway and asked her to tell them all about it. She continue to maintain that she had never seen a gun in the house, but her eyes kept flicking to her bed and the canny detective told his men to search it. In between the mattresses, they found a single-barrelled shotgun that had recently been fired.

Jane knew it was all up. She told McCarthy she had been arguing with her nephew for some weeks before the murder. She claimed he wanted her to leave, but refused to compensate her for the many years of keeping the house or the money she had invested in the place. Jane confessed to taking her nephew's gun and lying in wait to shoot him, but said she had only wanted 'to give him a fright tonight for what he said to me'.

The trial took place on 6 June 1932 in the Central Criminal Court in Dublin. Such a large crowd turned up to see the 60-year-old woman who had coldly killed her nephew that people had to be turned away from the packed courthouse. Jane O'Brien was found guilty and sentenced to death, but she was reprieved a week before the scheduled execution and had her sentence commuted to life imprisonment.

While in prison, Jane O'Brien sought part of the estate of the nephew she had killed, but, unsurprisingly, her claim was denied. She was released from Mountjoy Prison in July 1941 to the care of the Sisters of Charity of St Vincent de Paul, who ran Our Lady's Home on Henrietta Street in Dublin, where she remained for the rest of her life. When a former neighbour visiting Dublin called in to the convent to see her, Jane was eager to hear news of her old neighbours, and only briefly referred to the murder 'as the time I left home'.

The Axe-Woman of Fedamore

On 5 August 1925, Annie Walshe of Carnane, Fedamore, County Limerick earned the dubious distinction of becoming the only woman to be executed by the Irish state. She had murdered her husband with the help of his nephew.

Sometime after 7am on 25 October 1924, Annie Walshe arrived at the Fedamore Garda barracks and told shocked officers that her husband had been dragged out of bed near midnight and shot by his nephew, Michael Talbot, outside in a field. Annie had a small bruise under her left eye and told them Talbot had hit her and held her down for the entire night. Gardaí already knew there had been friction between Michael Talbot and Annie Walshe. Talbot only recently had been released from Limerick prison after serving six months for assaulting her.

When gardaí arrived at Walshe's home, they found 60-year-old Edward Walshe lying in a pool of blood in front of the fireplace. The dead man was fully dressed, with his cap on, wearing a pair of boots. They immediately were suspicious of 31-year-old Annie Walshe, but did not arrest her on the spot. Instead, they methodically spent the day examining the crime scene and interviewing neighbours.

Edward Walshe's sister Alice lived close by and she said Annie had come to her door at 7am shouting. She said

22-year-old Michael Talbot had come to the house, dragged 'Ned' out to the field and shot him dead, and added that she was going to the guards. Alice testified that she had not heard shots and no other neighbours had either.

Dr W. Hederman from Croom examined the body, looking for the bullet wound, but was unable to find it. Instead, he found that Edward Walshe had suffered skull fractures in two places and had died from these wounds, which had been caused by the blow of a heavy instrument. Dr Hederman searched the room, but did not find a bullet or any evidence of a ricochet.

Gardaí on the scene noted Annie's strange behaviour. Sergeant Kenny of Fedamore recorded that she had asked, 'Will I get compensation for him?' Superintendent Millard of Croom went to investigate the murder and met Annie at the house. She was perfectly calm and said, 'I am waiting for the cheque for him.' He thought she was referring to burial money and did not pay much attention at the time. Garda Maguire of Fedamore corroborated Sergeant Kenny's evidence and added that Annie had told him, 'I am rid of the Walshes now, and I will go back to my own people.' These were hardly the words of a grieving widow.

Michael Talbot lived nearby in a small cottage. Gardaí discovered him there shortly before midnight on 25 October and arrested him hiding there for murdering Edward Walshe. On being charged, Talbot told them: 'You may arrest Mrs Walshe as well as me.' He claimed she had killed his uncle with a hatchet. 'I held his hands while she killed him. She struck him two blows and he died.' Talbot continued: 'Wasn't she to get £20 over the last case! She was to divide it with me. She expected to get compensation for Ned. I was to keep away until she got the money, and we were then to go away together. I will show you the hatchet she killed him with.' Talbot said he stayed all night in bed with Annie after the murder, until 6.30am.

The gardaí were shocked by what they had heard. Talbot had admitted to having an affair with his aunt and being involved in his uncle's murder. They brought him to the Walshe house, where the wake for Edward had started, and Talbot pointed out the larger of two hatchets as the murder weapon Annie had used to kill her husband. She was arrested and cautioned.

'I did not kill my husband,' she said. 'I swear that.'

'You did. You killed him with a hatchet,' Talbot said.

'You are a liar. You killed him,' Annie said.

'That is the hatchet you killed him with,' Talbot said, indicating the tool.

'Talbot told me not to say anything about this,' Annie told the gardaí, 'and I said I would not.'

The two accused were brought to William Street station, but at first neither made a statement about the murder. In the evening, gardaí brought them together to see what would happen, and they were not disappointed. Talbot said he wanted to make a statement and did so in Annie's presence. He told them he had met Annie on 23 October and she had told him to come over the next night and they would kill her husband. She said she would get compensation for his death and would give Talbot half the money.

Talbot went over at 10pm, and while they sitting at the fire, Annie told Edward to go out for some sticks. While he was outside she put a hatchet under her apron and lowered the oil lamp. When Edward returned she hit him on the head with the hatchet. She told Talbot to restrain Edward and then struck her husband another blow. After that, Edward did not stir any more. Talbot remained with Annie until the morning, when she told him she would go for the gardaí, and warned him not to let them see him.

While Talbot was making his statement, Annie kept interrupting, saying he was lying. She too made a statement. This time Talbot interrupted her as she spoke. Annie said he had arrived at the house drunk, forced in the door, entered the kitchen and produced a revolver. He had knocked down her husband and then shot him in the head. Talbot had then told her not to stir, and held her down by the throat all night, threatening her if she went to the gardaí. Talbot protested that he had not been drunk and had never carried a revolver in his life.

The pair went on trial for the murder together in Limerick, but a jury could not produce a verdict and a retrial was ordered. This too failed to produce a verdict and the case went to the Central Criminal Court in Dublin. This time Michael Talbot and Annie Walshe were tried separately. Michael went on trial on 9 July 1925 and Annie the following day. The juries were instructed that it did not matter who had delivered the fatal blows to Edward Walshe – if they believed the murder had been carried out by both defendants acting together, each was as guilty as the other.

Evidence and testimony from witnesses were heard by the court on each day, and the case against the pair damned them both. Michael Talbot's statement was the more credible one, but it was an admission of guilt as well as a condemnation of Annie. Perhaps he had reasoned that he might receive a lesser sentence by saying he had only held Edward's hands, while she had killed him.

Annie Walshe's statement was riven with untruths. For example, a neighbour had met Michael Talbot as he had arrived at the Walshe's at 10pm, not near midnight as she claimed. The neighbour also testified that Talbot had not been drunk. Annie had said that Talbot gained entry to the house after knocking and pushing in the jamb, saying, 'You were very hard on me at the last court day and now it is time to have revenge.' But gardaí could find no evidence that the door had been forced in. Annie's claim that her husband had been shot was clearly a blatant lie too.

The juries quickly found both Annie Walshe and Michael Talbot guilty of the murder, and they were sentenced to death. They were executed at Mountjoy Prison on 5 August 1925 by English hangman Thomas Pierpoint. His normal fee for travelling to Ireland to conduct an execution was £10, but in this case the authorities bargained him down to £15 for the two.

The La Mancha Massacre

The murder of six people in a house near Malahide, County Dublin in 1926 caused a sensation at the time. At 8am on 31 March of that year, Henry McCabe arrived to work in the gardens at La Mancha, a large Georgian country house set in thirty acres of land. He quickly saw that smoke was billowing out of the house and realised it was on fire. He set off for Malahide at once to raise the alarm.

La Mancha was home to the McDonnell family, four middle-aged, unmarried siblings in their forties and fifties – Peter, Joseph, Alice and Annie. Two servants also lived in the house. James Clarke was a jack of all trades and indispensable aide to the family, and Mary McGowan was a maid. The family had previously lived in Ballygar, County Galway, where they had run the family business, a successful general store that had sold everything from groceries to hardware. They had sold the business and moved with Clarke to the house outside the thriving town of Malahide six years earlier, and settled down to a genteel life. A few weeks before the tragedy, the family had put up La Mancha and its prime lands for sale.

Sergeant Kenny and two other Malahide gardaí were first to arrive on the scene at 8.30am. Before the fire brigade arrived, Sergeant Kenny broke through the barred basement window of a room that was not on fire and discovered the body of James Clarke, partially dressed, on his bed. Police dragged him out the window and laid him on the lawn. On his head was a gaping wound from the blow of a heavy instrument like a poker or axe, and it was later said it would have dropped him 'like an ox'. There was no sign of a struggle or blood on the floor, suggesting that Clarke – a well-built man – had been killed somewhere else.

Firefighters arrived at 9am, but by that time most of the roof had fallen in and all the rooms of the ground floor were on fire. Meanwhile, Sergeant Kenny had gone into the room above the one Clarke had been in and found the body of Peter McDonnell. He too had been killed by a blow to the head. The room was not on fire, but paraffin had been spread about. The body lay on the bed naked, but a singlet and underwear had been draped over it. This body was also taken from the house and laid on the lawn.

Firefighters continued to battle the blaze, and they discovered the badly burnt bodies of Alice and Annie McDonnell and Mary McGowan in a bedroom. The fire damage made it impossible to tell if they too had been killed by blows to the head. In another room, the body of Joseph McDonnell was discovered. He too was badly burned and it was not possible to say if fractures to his skull had been caused before or after his death.

Soon, all six bodies were laid beside each other on the lawn, and the mystery of their deaths remained to be solved. A post-mortem examination discovered the presence of arsenic in each of the bodies. The six victims had been given quantities that were not enough to kill them, but would have made them ill and incapacitated them. They had been dead at least a day or two.

From the outset it was clear that whoever had killed all six people knew them and La Mancha intimately, and the person who fitted this description best was the gardener, Henry McCabe. The 48-year-old Wicklow man had worked at La Mancha for nine years and was happy there. He lived in Malahide with his wife and nine children. The last time anyone from the household had been seen by anyone but the gardener was at 4pm on 29 March. Alice had called into a dressmakers in Malahide but had to hurry home as Annie was unwell – presumably from poisoning.

McCabe made a detailed statement to the gardaí on 2 April in which he claimed that the family had been acting strange in the previous few weeks and described instances of individual members' odd acts. He also said James Clarke had been talking to himself for some weeks before the fire, and that the sale of the house had preyed on Clarke's mind. McCabe's statement was recorded as an attempt to suggest that one of the household had killed the others and themselves. Had the fire consumed the house, this explanation might have been accepted.

While gardaí examined Clarke's room again, McCabe went off somewhere. He returned ten minutes later with a set of keys to the family's safe, which he said he had found upstairs in a pair of trousers. He later said gardaí had asked him to look for a set of keys, but they denied this. When the safe was opened, it was found to be practically empty, although it had been estimated to contain a small fortune. Gardaí suspected McCabe had cleared it out.

McCabe was arrested for the murders on 12 April 1926 and stool trial on 6 November 1926. The trial lasted six days, and more than sixty witnesses testified. A detective gave evidence of encountering McCabe on the morning of the fire. 'This is an awful business,' the detective said, and McCabe replied, 'It is, and I after being up all night. They were all right when I left here last night, and when I got here this morning, I got an awful fright: the back door was broken in.'

The back door was indeed broken, but gardaí noted that it had been damaged on the inside. On the same morning, McCabe had been found to be wearing a pair of new, grey trousers that had belonged to Peter McDonnell. On the day he was charged with the murders, a garda named Hayden spoke with him and asked how he was. Hayden told the court McCabe replied, 'It is all up with me now. I am going to Mountjoy in the morning, and it is all over the pants I have on me. Would I be able to get out and tell my wife to say I got the pants some time ago in a parcel which the McDonnells sent me?'

The prosecution showed that McCabe had had ample time and opportunity to carry out the killings and was the only one who could have done it. He was the only person known to have been in the house between late 29 March and the time the fire was reported, and he had been at La Mancha all day on each of the four days leading up to 31 March. Between the time Alice McDonnell had been in Malahide on the afternoon of 29 March and the morning of the fire, three people had called to La Mancha and the only person they had met was McCabe.

Mrs O'Reilly, who lived in La Mancha's gate lodge, had called up at 4.30pm on 29 March to leave a parcel of bacon, but got no reply at the house. She had met McCabe, who told her that everyone was sick and James Clarke had been away since 27 March. Peter McDonnell usually gave her a shopping list for the household on Tuesdays, but on 28 March McCabe came down with the order instead. This had never happened before. As McCabe left, he told her not to bother to bring them up, as he would come down for them later.

At 2.30pm on the same day a water meter reader arrived, could not gain admittance and left when McCabe appeared and told him the family was sick. Two young girls selling raffle tickets to an upcoming fête in Malahide also called to the house. McCabe answered the door and bought some tickets.

When McCabe took the stand he said the gardaí had made up his statements. Two women, neighbours of McCabe's, testified to meeting Peter McDonnell in Malahide on the evening of 30 March, and the judge later advised the jury to acquit McCabe if they believed their evidence, as it was the prosecution's case that the deaths had occurred well before the alleged meeting.

In summing up, the judge mentioned the importance of the demeanour of these witnesses and of McCabe – in other words, whether they were believable. The jury thought not, and found McCabe guilty after less than an hour of deliberations. When asked why he should not be sentenced to death, McCabe said, 'All I have to say is God forgive them. I am the victim of bribery and perjury.' As his death sentence was passed, McCabe stood ashen-faced, right hand gripping the bar of the dock. While he was being led away, it appeared that he was starting to cry.

McCabe was executed in Mountjoy Prison at 8am on 9 December 1926. Among the crowd gathered outside the prison, which was two hundred or three hundred strong, were McCabe's wife and several of their children. When notice that the sentence had been carried out was posted outside the prison, she read it and 'wept bitterly'.

A few days later, an article in the *Sunday Independent* revealed that McCabe had once been convicted of trying to kill a girlfriend and had been jailed for fifteen months. The same article said the fires at La Mancha had been starved of oxygen. Had some windows been open, the house and any evidence in it would have been destroyed and McCabe might never have been caught.

It was never clear what McCabe's motive had been for the killings. Had the sale of La Mancha, and an uncertain future if the new owners let him go, prompted McCabe's terrible actions?

The Seskin Sensation

James McCalmont, a young farm labourer, was driving his cart from Straid to collect milk on the morning of 4 September 1931 as usual when his horse began shying and refused to go any further. Looking over the roadside wall at Seskin, near Carrickfergus, County Antrim, where the horse had stopped, McCalmont saw the partially concealed body of a man, naked except for a blue-and-white bathing cap on his head.

McCalmont immediately headed for the Carrickfergus police station to report his discovery. After police searched and recorded the scene, the body was removed to a mortuary. A post-mortem examination revealed that death had taken place some ten hours previously and the victim had been killed by two shots to the head from a .25-caliber pistol. The unknown victim was six feet two inches tall and was in his late thirties. There were no clues as to his identity.

A bundle of bloodstained clothes had been found the day before in a gateway in Church Lane in Belfast. When newspapers reported the corpse's discovery, the clothing was taken to the police. It included a blue waterproof coat, trousers and a jacket, all of which had been roughly cut up. Police speculated that the clothes had been cut off the mystery body in Carrickfergus to prevent his identification.

An investigation found that the mackintosh had been stolen from McIlroy's garage on Princes Street on 2 September. A shoe was found in an alleyway off Princes Street and turned out to belong to the victim.

The mystery man's picture was published in the *Belfast Telegraph* to help identify him, and police learned that a Belfast woman had been keeping company with two foreign visitors. Rose McGowan told police she had met them outside the Great Victoria Street Station on 29 August and struck up a conversation. It had been arranged that they would take McGowan and her friend Peggie Murphy to Bangor the following day in their car. One was an American who called himself Bernard Berman, and the other was a tall Turk called Achmet Musa. The party of four set out from Ryan's Hotel on 30 August.

With the body identified as Achmet Musa, detectives delved into his past. His story began in Istanbul, where he had been a servant of one Zaro Agha, who claimed to be 156 years old. A bright Turkish showman named Assim Redvan had the idea of styling Agha as 'the world's oldest man' and exploiting him as a fairground attraction in the English-speaking world. The trio went to America to get backing.

There they met a 28-year-old Cypriot Jew called Eddie Cullens, who had settled in America and had extensive connections. He thought Zaro Agha had commercial potential and agreed to promote him. The four men arrived in England in the spring of 1931 and persuaded Bertram Mills Circus to take on Agha as a sideshow for a tour of the countryside. However, the circus' manager was only willing to hire Agha and Redvan, and the four men had to split the proceeds between them. Was this why Achmet Musa had been murdered?

Investigators learned that Cullens had rented a house in Liverpool for two weeks in August under the name Bernard Berman, giving a false address in Southport. They also learned that Cullens had inquired about renting a lock-up garage. He had asked what kind of floor it had, and when he was told that it had an earthen floor, he had said that was perfect as he wanted to repair his car. When the garage owner asked whether he was with the circus, 'Berman' pointedly said he was not.

On 26 August, the garage owner was passing by the premises when he noticed it was not padlocked and went to investigate. He tried the door and discovered it was secured from the inside. He shouted through it, asking who inside. A few moments later, a sweating Berman opened the door, came out and got permission to put his own lock on the door.

On 28 August, Cullens and Musa borrowed an Essex saloon car from Assim Redvan and took the night ferry from Liverpool to Belfast. On arrival in Belfast the next morning, they arranged lodgings in Ryan's Hotel on Donegal Quay. Later that afternoon, Cullens chatted up McGowan outside the train station, and the next day the foursome set out for Bangor.

Cullens, who was driving, stopped along the way at a garage to have a tyre changed. After this had been done, he washed his hands at the garage. Returning to the car, he reached into a door pocket and pulled out two towels, a pair of gloves and a distinctive blue-and-white bathing cap. The next day, the men drove McGowan to Londonderry to visit her family. They waited around for a while, but when she did not return at the agreed time they returned to Belfast without her.

On 2 September, Cullens and Musa paid their bill at Ryan's around 6pm and departed. An hour later, Matthew Ryan met them on Donegal Quay. He walked with them to McIlroy's garage to pick up their car and they gave Ryan a lift to the Albert Memorial, where they dropped him on his way to attend the greyhound racing at Celtic Park. Ryan last saw them driving along Corporation Street heading for Carrickfergus, he later told police.

Detectives could not find anyone – besides Cullens – who saw Musa alive after this point. At midnight that day, Cullens was seen near Seskin, sitting in his distinctive Essex saloon, which was blocking the road. Another driver told police he had stopped and talked with Cullens there that night. Police surmised that Musa was dead by this time and thought Cullens must have then driven back to Belfast with Musa's bloody clothes.

Police established that Cullens arrived back in Liverpool on the morning of 4 September. He went to the owner of the house he had been renting to pick up his and Musa's things, explaining that his friend was not coming back. He told the circus manager that Musa had met a woman in Londonderry and had remained behind. Cullens later told a girlfriend in London that Musa had been shipped back to Turkey because he had threatened Zaro Agha.

Police later tracked down Eddie Cullens when the circus was in Leeds. Among his belongings was the case of a distinctive pistol that used the same .25-caliber ammunition that killed Musa. The two towels and gloves were found in the car, but the bathing cap was missing. Police arrested Cullens and charged him with the murder of his fellow showman.

The trial took place at Armagh on 8 December 1931. Cullens pleaded not guilty. The prosecution told the court that police had opened the Liverpool garage Cullens had rented and found a new pickaxe and shovel. They suggested that he had been planning to dig a grave in the garage to dispose of Musa's body. When he had been disturbed, Cullens had decided to take his victim to Northern Ireland and kill him there instead.

The most important witnesses at the trial were Sarah and Matthew Ryan, who both testified that neither Musa nor Cullens had stayed at their hotel on the night of 2 September. Cullens later claimed they were wrong, but the Ryans were adamant. A clerk at the Belfast Steamship Company produced records showing that a man called Barney Berman had gone to their office on the morning of 3 September to book a car on the ferry to Liverpool. He identified Cullens as the man who had made the booking.

Cullens took the stand and explained that he had lied about his occupation when renting the house in Liverpool, as it was difficult to find accommodation as a circus person. He denied renting the garage under the name Berman, saying he had given Redvan's name as Redvan had asked him to find a garage for his new car. He also denied asking about the garage's floor. Cullens claimed Redvan had told him to buy the pickaxe and shovel for their tent, as they had been plagued by flooding and wanted to dig a trench outside it.

When asked why they had gone to Ireland, Cullens explained that Musa had had a fight with a circus person and he had been asked to take him away for a few days. Redvan had lent him the car and they had gone to Ireland for a short break. Cullens dismissed the two girls' testimony. He said McGowan had spoken against him because he had left her in Londonderry, and that there had been no bathing cap in the car.

Cullens testified that he had spent the evening of 2 September with Matthew Ryan at the dog track, had returned to the car afterwards and had found Musa missing. Musa had not shown up at the hotel, and Cullen had left the next day for Liverpool with his belongings. Assim Redvan gave evidence on Cullens' behalf, and corroborated his story.

The prosecution told the court that Redvan had called at Ryan's Hotel on 4 November and tried to persuade them to say that Cullens had stayed there on 2 September. Redvan said he had merely wanted to find out if Cullens had stayed there on 2 September and had told the Ryans to tell the truth.

After a three-day trial, and a valiant effort by Cullens to avoid his fate, it took the jury only a little over half an hour to find him guilty. He was hanged at Belfast Prison on 13 January 1932.

Solved by a Dream

Adam Rogers, who kept a public house at Portlaw, County Waterford, in 1759 dreamed that he saw one man murder another at a particular green spot on a nearby mountain. The victim was small and sickly, the killer large and strong. The vivid dream disturbed Rogers. He told his wife and several neighbours about it next morning.

After some time he went out coursing with greyhounds in company with friends, including the local priest, Father Browne. When they stopped at the green spot on the mountain, Rogers told Father Browne about his terrible dream. He thought little more about it for the rest of the day, but the next morning Rogers was startled to see a pair resembling the men in his dream come into the public house.

He ran and told his wife, and the couple kept a close watch on the men. The small man, a quiet and gentle soul named James Hickey, and was returning home a wealthy man to his family after many years abroad. His companion was called Frederick Caulfield, and had a 'ferocious bad countenance'. They had met on the way back to Ireland and become friends.

The publican did not like the look of Caulfield, and he tried to persuade Hickey to stay, saying he would accompany him to Carrick-on-Suir the following day. But Caulfield convinced Hickey to continue on, and Rogers could do

James Hickey is murdered by Frederick Caulfield.

nothing. He was too embarrassed to tell Hickey about the dream. Rogers' wife was furious when she found out that the two men were gone, and she blamed her husband for not doing more to detain Hickey.

An hour after leaving Portlaw, the men reached the lonely part of the mountain that Rogers had dreamed of. Here Caulfield murdered Hickey and stole his money. According to Caulfield, he waited until Hickey was crossing a ditch and hit the poor man on the head with a large stone. When Hickey fell into the ditch, Caulfield stabbed him several times and cut his throat so violently that his head was almost severed from his body. He then rifled through Hickey's pockets, took some of his clothes and everything else of value, and proceeded to Carrick. The body was still warm when it was discovered by local labourers returning to their work from dinner a short time later.

When they heard that a body had been discovered, Rogers and his wife went to the spot and identified the corpse. They were able to provide a good description of Caulfield and tell of their suspicions. Two days later, he was arrested in Waterford while attempting to get passage in the first ship leaving port. At Caulfield's trial, Adam Rogers and his wife were the main witnesses, but there was other testimony too: after killing Hickey, Caulfield had continued to Carrick and then doubled back towards Waterford by a back road. When his guide, a young boy, noticed blood on Caulfield's clothes, he was bribed to keep quiet.

The Rogerses gave a detailed description and account of Hickey and Caulfield. They proved that Caulfield had taken a new pair of shoes that Hickey had been wearing and put his old shoes on the corpse. Adam Rogers described in great detail every article of clothing the men wore. Caulfield shrewdly cross-examined Rogers from the dock and asked if it was not extraordinary that Rogers, the owner of a busy public house, would have paid such close attention to how strangers had dressed.

Rogers said he had had a particular interest in the men, but he was too ashamed to admit why. Caulfield and the judge insisted he state his reason, forcing Rogers to relate his foreboding dream. Rogers called on Father Browne, who was in the court, to corroborate his testimony, and said his wife had severely reprimanded him for allowing Hickey to leave the premises, knowing that on their way to Carrick the men would have to pass the green spot on the mountain that he had dreamed about.

The jury found Caulfield guilty of murder and the judge sentenced him to death. Caulfield then admitted his guilt.

While he was on his way home from two decades in the West Indies, carrying a large sum of money, Hickey's ship had taken shelter from stormy weather at Minch Head in Newfoundland. There he had befriended Caulfield, a sailor and fellow countryman, who had fallen on hard times. Hickey charitably relieved Caulfield's distress, it was agreed that they would continue on to Ireland together and Hickey paid his fellow Irishman's fare.

A witness said Caulfield frequently spoke poorly of the Good Samaritan who had been so kind to him. He was heard to say that it was a pity that such a puny fellow should have money while he himself was without a shilling. When they landed at Waterford, the pair remained together, and Hickey continued to foot all their expenses. It is said that Caulfield walked to the gallows 'with a firm step and undaunted countenance'.